King Solomon's Secret

by

Paul Anthony González

King Solomon's Secret

by

Paul Anthony González

Printed by KDP, An Amazon.com Company.

Available from Amazon.com and other retail outlets.

First Edition

Copyright © 2017

ISBN 13: 979-8-9877912-0-2

Cover Design by: Jessica Befera for FCI Brands

All rights reserved. No part of this publication may be reproduced or transmitted in any form or by any means, electronic or mechanical, including photocopy, recording, or any information storage retrieval system, without permission in writing from the copyright owner.

Scripture quotations marked (NLT) are taken from the Holy Bible, New Living Translation, copyright © 1996, 2004, 2007 by Tyndale House Foundation. Used by permission of Tyndale House Publishers, Inc., Carol Stream, Illinois 60188. All rights reserved.

Scripture taken from the New King James Version®. Copyright © 1982 by Thomas Nelson. Used by permission. All rights reserved.

Scripture quotations taken from the Amplified® Bible (AMP), Copyright © 2015 by The Lockman Foundation
Used by permission. www.Lockman.org

Scripture quotations marked (KJV) are taken from the King James Version of the Holy Bible.

Dedication

To my bride, Amy.
My first book is ours.
Thank you for always believing in my dreams.
You are the embodiment of Proverbs 18:22.

Acknowledgements

I would like to acknowledge and say thank you to Freedom House Church for sharing me with this writing project—your faith is evident to all. Dad, thank you for reading portions of this book and being such an inspiration. Mom, thank you for always encouraging me. Donna Porter and Bonnie Nielson read parts of the book and gave me honest feedback. Brian Schreiber helped with dates and timelines. Ken Porter sent a text message that inspired my favorite chapter. Christopher, Brittany, Jordan, David and Joshua are the greatest siblings a man could ask for. Thaddaeus, Jerund, Talia-Noelle, Brooklyn, Noah, Barak, Elisha, Pauly, Rachel and David provided me with the impetus I need every day to succeed in my calling and finish the race well. Wally and Lourdes gave me a month of unhindered creativity by being amazing hosts at Surfside Beach, SC. Lastly, Greg Baker of Affordable Christian Editing was a Godsend. His editorial expertise has made me a better writer.

Table of Contents

Chapter 1 – King Solomon's Secret 1
Chapter 2 – The Secret That Saved Me 23
Chapter 3 – The Secret That Hounded Me 36
Chapter 4 – Solomon's Secret Resting on a Region 50
Chapter 5 – Startling Encounters of a Secret Kind 68
Chapter 6 – The Secret Motivator 80
Chapter 7 – Jesus, on King Solomon's Secret 102
Chapter 8 – The Secret Ingredient to Successful Prayer 127
Chapter 9 – Seven Secret Steps to Successful Prayer 161
Chapter 10 – Final Thoughts on King Solomon's Secret 205
About the Author 223

— Paul Anthony González —

Chapter One
King Solomon's Secret

Growing up as the son of a prestigious king would be a tremendous burden for anyone to carry, especially if your mother became the king's wife after a scandalous affair. Solomon, son of the famed King David of Israel, had the pressure of following his father, a beloved national leader, and living with the burdensome knowledge that his father had his mother's first husband killed after impregnating her in an adulterous tryst.

King David was known to be a man that possessed the heart of a champion and a heart for God. From the time that he had defeated the infamous Philistine warrior-champion, Goliath of Gath, David ascended to the tops of the hearts of his people while climbing the ranks of political might and power. Though King David suffered incredible setbacks and moral failings, he always humbled himself, appealed for mercy, and returned to His God. God continued to undergird David with His loving favor, even after severely disciplining him.

Regarded as his most despicable error, David murdered a man in an attempt to take the man's wife. Rather than be on the field of battle with his army, like he had done in times past, David decided to stay home and scan the female community ceremonial cleansing pools from his roof top. It was his personal peep show, except the women were unwitting victims of his pornographic escapades. While indulging his sexual desires one afternoon, he spied an exceptionally lovely woman named Bathsheba. His desire to have her exceeded his ability to think rationally, and knowing she was married, he brought her home and had intercourse with her (2 Samuel 11:1-5).

A short time after their night of passion, Bathsheba secretly sent David a note letting him know that she had become pregnant. David panicked. To try and cover his sin, David decided to bring Uriah, Bathsheba's husband, home from his service in the army. Uriah was serving with the Jewish army in their war effort against the nation of Ammon. When Uriah arrived home, David inquired about the success of the army and then encouraged Uriah to go home and see his wife. David hoped that Uriah, who surely missed his beautiful bride, would have sex with her. David's plan failed (2 Samuel 11:5-8).

Uriah, rather than go home, stayed the night in front of the king's castle. When asked why he refused to go home and spend time with his wife, he replied that he would not—not as long as the rest of the able-bodied men of Israel were off at war. Uriah was an honorable man. David tried a second time to get Uriah to go home, even resorting to getting Uriah exceedingly drunk in another failed attempt (2 Samuel 11:9-13).

Seeing that Uriah was not going to go home and lay with Bathsheba, David sent him back to the battle. David was possessed with a desire to keep his adultery hidden (a severe breach of God's holy Ten Commandments and regarded as a deplorable act in Israel), so he ordered his war general, Joab, to move Uriah to the fiercest area of the battle lines. Then, in the midst of the fighting,

Joab was to withdraw his troops and leave Uriah alone in the fray to die. Joab obeyed and Uriah was killed. David's plan succeeded…or so David thought (2 Samuel 11:14-17; Exodus 20:14).

David waited for Bathsheba to take the customary time for mourning and then took her to be his wife. He believed he had gotten away with murder, but around the time the child was to be delivered, the Prophet Nathan came to confront David about his secrets. David was exposed, and he confessed his sin. He felt as though his secret was killing him slowly, and he was glad to be outed. Nathan reminded David that God was forgiving and merciful and that his sin was forever put away. However, since David had disgraced the name of God before Israel and before the eyes of the surrounding heathen nations, David would have to pay a hefty price, and pay he did. Bathsheba's child would have to die for David's crimes, and David's kingdom would be subject to constant turmoil from that time forward. It was an incredible payment for what he had done, but David took his punishment humbly and respectfully (2 Samuel 11:27-12:1-19).

David and Bathsheba were devastated by the loss of their infant child. A short time later, however, Bathsheba became pregnant again, and she successfully carried the child to term and delivered a healthy male child whom they named Solomon. Solomon's name means *peace,* and God made it clear that He loved Solomon. It was an incredible act of mercy toward David and Bathsheba to have God express His favor and acceptance of their new infant. It is a marvelous thing that God takes our failings and turns them for His good (2 Samuel 12:24-25).

However, during Solomon's upbringing, he was exposed to the often dark and painful side of governmental leadership, which included family in-fighting, power grabs, murderous plots, and other schemes. One brother, Absalom, who was enraged by his half-brother Amnon's rape of his sister Tamar—and consequently David's half-hearted discipline of Amnon for the deplorable act—had Amnon killed and attempted a near successful coup d'état. Solomon, along with his parents, had to flee Jerusalem and live on the run. Absalom held an orgy with his father's concubines on the very rooftop that David originally lusted after Bathsheba's nakedness (2 Samuel 13 - 20).

Eventually, the rebellion was squelched, and Absalom was killed by David's commander, Joab, against David's wishes. The deaths of his two sons, Amnon and Absalom, shattered David down to his soul, and he never fully recovered emotionally from it. Solomon witnessed the harsh realities of the resulting effect of his father's sin, and it no doubt had a profound impact upon him.

King David died at the age of seventy, and Solomon, handpicked by God, succeeded him. The Bible never tells us the exact age of Solomon when he ascended the throne, and depending on what scholar is consulted, we can confidently place his age between twelve and twenty. However, there is no argument by any theologian against the fact that he eventually succeeded David in becoming king and that he was relatively young.

Solomon may have witnessed turmoil and heartbreak in the life and kingdom of His father David, but he inherited David's deep love for God. Solomon was known to follow, at the beginning of his reign, the statutes of God with care, and he was not afraid to honor the Lord with public displays of worship. He would eventually fulfill his dad's original desire to build God a permanent temple in Jerusalem, and it was an architectural marvel in which he spared no expense (1 Kings 1:32, 3:4, 6).

Prior to building the temple, the people of Israel worshipped in different locations, and the primary location was in a place called Gibeon, eight kilometers northwest of Jerusalem. Shortly after David's death and his ascension to the throne, Solomon visited Gibeon to offer a thousand burnt offerings. It was an incredible gift and sacrifice even for a king, and that evening, God appeared to him in a dream and said, "Ask! What shall I give you?" (1 Kings 3:5).

I can't imagine how I would have responded to so great a question while in my adolescence, but I am certain it would not have mirrored Solomon's. His request gives us an open window into the type of young man Solomon was. To his credit, King David had been able to rear a God-fearing son, despite his own mistakes and the additional difficulties that were so typical in the polygamist households of the Bible. I reckon that most young men might have asked the Lord for selfish things like fame, fortune and financial success, but not Solomon. His desire touched the heart of His Maker:

> "And Solomon said: 'You have shown great mercy to Your servant David my father, because he walked before You in truth, in righteousness, and in uprightness of heart with You; You have continued this great kindness for him, and You have given him a son to sit on his throne, as it is this day. Now, O Lord my God, You have made Your servant king instead of my father David, but I am a little child; I do not know how to go out or come in. And Your servant is in the midst of Your people whom You have chosen, a great people, too numerous to be numbered or

> counted. Therefore give to Your servant an understanding heart to judge Your people, that I may discern between good and evil. For who is able to judge this great people of Yours?'" – 1 Kings 3:6-7, NKJV

While a person is asleep, God is able to speak to their deepest places and get the most honest responses. It is while we are at rest that we are at our most vulnerable, open and unable to mask or hide our truest intentions. I cannot say conclusively, but I am certain that had Solomon had selfishness hidden in his heart, he would not have been able to request a selfless desire. If there had been in him hidden, buried and corrupt ambitions, God would have seen through his facade and would have likely called him on it, but God's answer is spectacular:

> "The speech pleased the Lord, that Solomon had asked this thing. Then God said to him: 'Because you have asked this thing, and have not asked long life for yourself, nor have asked riches for yourself, nor have asked the life of your enemies, but have asked for yourself understanding to discern justice, behold, I have done according to your words; see, I have given you a wise and understanding heart, so that there has not been anyone like you before you, nor shall any like you arise after you. And I have also given you what you have not asked: both riches and honor, so that there shall not be anyone like you among the kings all your days. So if you walk in My ways, to keep My statutes and My commandments, as your father David walked, then I will lengthen your days.'" – 1 Kings 3:10-14

While Solomon was asking for an *understanding heart*, he probably did not know that he would be immeasurably blessed beyond his wildest imagination. Not only did God satisfy his desire, but he added to it wisdom, fame, wealth, prestige, and, should he continue to be faithful to the commandments, long life.

The fame of Solomon's wisdom immediately spread far and wide throughout the nation, and the people loved their king. It was not long until his notoriety catapulted him into international acclaim. He became a highly sought out advisor, teacher and counselor to the kings of the earth. A queen from an east African nation, the Queen of Sheba, tested Solomon with "hard questions" and was moved, due to his accurate and wise answers, to share "all that was in her heart." Before she left Jerusalem to return to her own land and people, she attested to the fact that Solomon's fame was so unbelievably widespread that she simply had not believed the rumors that had come into her land. However, when she saw the order, peace and excellence of his government and nation, along with the wisdom, knowledge and understanding that poured from his heart, she was convinced that only "the half" had been told to her (2 Chronicles 9:23; 1 Kings 10:1-9).

Not only had Solomon arisen to international esteem and honor as God had promised he would, but he was an avid naturalist whose counsel on things pertaining to the cosmos was regarded and sought after as well. Additionally, he was a prolific writer of poetry, songs and proverbs, and he used his many precepts to share the wonderful and eternal truths of God. Many of his proverbs were recorded in two different books in the Bible: Proverbs and Ecclesiastes.

Solomon had also attained a vast trove of precious metals and gained great economic success both personally and nationally. He managed to set up very effective trade deals that provided his kingdom with a steady stream of income through tariffs and taxes. In spite of his financial status, Solomon did not lose sight of where and how his wealth had come. He did not forget that God had promised him that he would be made wealthy due to his request for wisdom and understanding. He learned that he had made the right decision in asking for wisdom, and it was wisdom that would gain him access to all earthly successes. Many times in his writings, he treated wisdom as a living being and referred to wisdom in the feminine gender. He said of lady wisdom that "Length of days is in her right hand, In her left hand riches and honor" (Proverbs 3:16).

Solomon had come to regard wisdom as more valuable than anything else that one could achieve, gain or accomplish. In fact, he wrote that "wisdom is more valuable than rubies. Nothing you desire can compare with it." The Hebrew to Greek rendering of the Old Testament, known as *The Septuagint*, translates the same verse into the English as: "For wisdom is better than precious stones, and no valuable substance is of equal worth with it" (Proverbs 8:11, NLT).

It is not uncommon for Christians to experience the very same challenges and difficulties as non-believers, and because we have an adversary that contests our faith, the devil/Satan, many times our trials are heightened. We suffer financial, relational and health related problems just as others do. We, on occasion, pray and see little results or changes and may feel that we have to grin and bear the burden. But what if we went about these challenges a little differently? What if we stopped simply seeing a *financial* problem and instead regarded it as a *wisdom* problem? If we could attain wisdom on the particular matter that is besetting us, then we would have the necessary information on how to solve it, and perhaps this is why Solomon admonishes his readers in Proverbs 4:5 to "Get wisdom!"

In the seventh verse of the same chapter, he points out that it is wisdom that "is the principle thing." Strangely, and remarkably silent, is the mention of prayer. He does not say that prayer is the principle thing. No, *wisdom* is. Here is a man that was graced by God supernaturally and endowed from on high to write and record eternal realities. Truths that transform. If he says that wisdom is the key issue in any situation, then we would be wise to listen. Prayer is vital, yet we often say words without any real focus and, consequently, any real power. What if we could pray with precision—with accuracy? Well, we can. It is called wisdom. We can face any challenge, any situation, any trial, and we can face them with confidence, because God, Solomon writes, has given us His wisdom, should we desire it.

Whatever one is chasing, whatever one is after, and whatever one is steering his family toward, it cannot compare to the acquisition of the treasure that is wisdom. Wisdom will guide in all good ways, right choices, and quality decisions. Wisdom will prosper beyond imagination and, with the prosperity, great contentment. We cannot understate the value of wisdom.

One afternoon, my mother informed my wife and I that she had been to the doctor for a checkup, and she'd been told that her calcium levels were above the normal range. The doctor informed her that he was not overly concerned, but if her levels did not normalize, then he would need to do some additional testing. She informed him that she had been taking a calcium supplement, and he asked her to quit. She complied. We prayed for her, and three months later, she went back to test her levels again. We were confident that the calcium levels would be within the normal range. They were not. They were still elevated to a point that caused the doctor great concern. He said that he would bring her back for additional tests and told her what the possible causes might be. We were greatly troubled.

That was when I shifted the way I had been praying. I reasoned that since the way I had been praying didn't adjust anything, then perhaps I should take a different approach. We had been praying for her levels to normalize and for the root cause to be eliminated. I decided to ask for *wisdom* concerning the matter. In my daily prayer times and throughout the day for a few days, I focused only on gaining supernatural insight, and I made sure to give my heart to listening to the Lord. After a few days, the Lord spoke to me. I did not hear an audible voice, and had anyone been near me, they would not have heard a voice either. However, I did hear Him as clear as day down in my heart, and He said these words to me: "Your mother drinks a lot of water. More than most people. Put a high quality water filter on her sink and make sure it filters out calcium, and her levels will normalize."

I obeyed immediately, and my mother also believed what the Lord had said to me. We ordered a high quality, triple-reverse-osmosis-filtration system for her main sink. She asked the doctor to delay the testing for a couple of months to see if her levels would go down, and when she went back for the tests, her levels were normal. Wisdom had properly directed us!

The Source of Divine Wisdom - Solomon's Secret Revealed

Diamonds are a highly valued and much sought after jewel. The most expensive diamond on earth is the Mountain of Light diamond which is the property of the British Crown. It is a one-hundred and five carat beauty and is considered priceless. It has never been estimated. In comparison, the Cullinan Diamond, also known as the Star of Africa, and weighing a staggering six-hundred and twenty-one grams is worth four-hundred million dollars! Imagine, for a moment, if you were the recipient of any one of these diamonds. What would you do with it? Would you sell it or save it and wait for it to increase in value? Having either one of the two diamonds would be an amazing retirement plan.

Diamonds are forged in the earth under intense heat and indescribable pressure. All of the Earth's diamonds, known and undiscovered, have formed over a period that is between twenty-five to seventy-five percent of the total age of the Earth. Their value is found, not only in their rarity, but also in the length of time it takes for them to be forged deep within the Earth's mantle. Additionally, the work that must go into finding diamonds, especially the most expensive ones, adds to their value, since it is an incredible undertaking. In fact, the colloquial expression, "like digging for diamonds," has become synonymous with the hard work, toil and patience it takes to accomplish a worthwhile dream or goal. Yet, as valuable as diamonds are, and in spite of the fact that most of us would love to be given a fistful of them, we do not *need* them to survive on a daily basis. We may never own a single diamond in the entirety of our lifetime, but we can still live a life of meaning and value. We do not need diamonds to live.

Most have never stopped to consider how valuable the Earth, from which diamonds are mined, actually is. Without the proper working of its ecosystems and the health of its water sources, mankind could not properly thrive. We take our planet for granted more often than not. For example, the destruction of our planet's lungs, the rain forests, and its continual deforestation have greatly diminished the absorption of greenhouse gasses and carbon dioxide, which is necessary for the production of oxygen. Without oxygen, nothing will live.

Mankind needs the Earth to remain healthy if we are to survive, and without it, there would be no humanity to speak of. As costly as diamonds are, their worth cannot compare to the value of the Earth. The foundation upon which a diamond is forged is the Earth, and therefore, we can rightly surmise that the foundation and source from which anything proceeds—in this case diamonds—is of greater intrinsic value than the thing that flows out from it. In other words, if there is no source, there can be no valuable resource. The Earth is more valuable than all of the diamonds combined.

With this thought in mind, consider Solomon's words in Proverbs 9:10: "**The fear of the Lord** is the beginning of wisdom."

The New Living translation of the same verse translates *beginning* as *foundation*, and the Amplified translation says that "the fear of the Lord" is the "starting point and essence of wisdom."

Wisdom is incredibly costly, but it cannot exceed the source from which it flows and is built upon, and that source is ***the*** *fear of the Lord*. Just as every person in possession of a precious jewel or metal must be thankful for the Earth from which they were found, so too must we look to the source of wisdom with the same sober reminder. The *fear of the Lord* is *King Solomon's Secret*.

If the Earth, God forbid, disintegrated, all of its diamonds would go with it. No earth—no diamonds. When the fear of God (I use *the fear of the Lord* and *the fear of God interchangeably*) erodes in a person, church or culture, so too does wisdom. It is more important for us to care for and steward our earth than it is to mine for gems, and it is more important that we cultivate a healthy respect for God than to crave the treasures of wisdom. Wisdom flows out from the fear of God, and when we maintain the fear of God, the treasures that wisdom produces will follow suit, because the fear of God is the source from which all of heaven's wisdom flows. We need to fear God to walk in great wisdom, live a long life, and enjoy riches and honor (Proverbs 10:27, 14:27, 19:23, 22:4).

The Sad Case of Losing the Secret

I wish that I could share that Solomon's life ended as excellently as it started, but sadly it did not. Solomon lost the fear of God and, with it, his ability to make wise decisions for himself and his nation. Solomon had an affinity for women—many women. It is highly probable that he had a sex addiction, but we cannot know for sure. It is because of his appetites that he began marrying, in direct contradiction to God's commandment, foreign women who worshipped idols and committed abominable sacrifices to them. His heart was taken captive by their beauty and by his carnal desires, and he began to worship the idols of his women right alongside of them. He "clung to these women in love…and his heart was not loyal to the Lord his God, as was the heart of his father David" (1 Kings 11:2,4; Deuteronomy 17:17).

Hosea 4:11 (KJV) says, "Whoredom and wine and new wine take away the heart." It was Solomon who admonished in the fourth chapter of Proverbs and the 23rd verse (NKJV) to "Keep your heart with all diligence, For out of it *spring* the issues of life," so it is both sad and surprising that he allowed his heart to be seduced and ultimately taken away because of a penchant for sex with many different women—women who worshiped other gods.

The net result of whoredom and habitual imbibing is that the heart will begin to grow cold toward the things of God, and the fear of the Lord will be especially affected by this. I have witnessed, time and time-again, men and women who were hot for the things of God, but who, through the continual indulgence of perverse living, steadily fell away as their heart became numb. Solomon's heart was no different.

He started making poor choices—his wisdom was fading—and he began building high places for he and his women to hold sacrifices, sexual orgies, and human sacrifices. Solomon married a Moabite woman and he built Chemosh, the national god of Moab, a place for additional human sacrifice. The Moabites were descendants of Lot, the nephew of the great patriarch Abraham. When Lot was fleeing the divine overthrow of Sodom and Gomorrah, he hid out in a nearby mountain where he became extremely drunk and had sex with both of his daughters. The disgusting practices of the foul city in which he was a former resident had rubbed off on him and his girls, and they committed an extremely lewd act. One of his daughters gave birth to Moab, and his offspring became the sworn enemies and a constant threat of the Israelites. God called their god the "abomination of Moab" (1Kings 11:1-8; Genesis 19).

The New Testament book of 1 Corinthians warns against the practice of fornication: "Know ye not that he which is joined to an harlot is one body? for two, saith he, shall be one flesh" (1 Corinthians 6:16, KJV). The warning is due in part to the very spiritual aspects of sexual union. Many people are not aware that they take on, in a sense, the nature, attitudes and spiritual condition of the person they have been intimate with. That is why a Christian must never marry a person outside of their faith, because doing so, will cause continual spiritual and emotional turmoil, turmoil that has little remedy outside of an unbelieving person finally surrendering to Christ. Solomon became the very thing he was intimate with, and the fear of God left him. With it went the wisdom he had been famous for. Without wisdom operating in our lives, we are destined for repeated failures. We must get wisdom, and when we have it, we must keep it, but to do so, we cannot forfeit the fear of God.

Solomon had enjoyed uncommon peace with his neighboring nations, and many of them were allied with him, but after his moral decline, God permitted adversaries to beset his realm. His nation began to fracture, and it was God who told him that he had, as a result of his sin, permitted the eventual northern rebellion and civil war of his nation. God had desired to keep Israel unified, but Solomon had welcomed demonic forces to stew within the culture, and there would have to be a reckoning (1 Kings 11:11).

In what would be an extremely bad leadership decision, Solomon handpicked a young man named Jeroboam to be his officer over all of his labor force in building up a fortification near

Jerusalem. Jeroboam fomented rebellion due to the excessively deplorable conditions of the work hours, pay and environment. The Queen of Sheba had once remarked on the happiness of Solomon's servants, but their happiness was no doubt turned to resentment along with the turning of Solomon's heart away from the fear of God. Jeroboam would fracture the Kingdom of Israel irreparably during the reign of Solomon's son, Rehoboam (1 Kings 11:26-43; 1 Kings 14:30).

A Sobering Rediscovery of the Secret

The Old Testament proverbial book of Ecclesiastes has a sober, somber and somewhat depressive tone to it. Although the work is attributed to Solomon, some scholars doubt that Solomon wrote it. Ecclesiastes is written in a tenor that is uniquely different from his love ballad of The Song of Solomon and his writings in the book of Proverbs. An oft repeated word in Ecclesiastes, depending on what version is referenced, is *vanity*. For example, in the second verse of the opening chapter, the writer pronounces, "Vanity of vanities, saith the Preacher, vanity of vanity; all is vanity," and in another place he decries life as "vanity and vexation of spirit" (Ecclesiastes 1:14, KJV).

It is not improbable that Solomon wrote the book because the writer makes the self-describing statement: "Look, I have attained greatness, and have gained more wisdom than all who were before me in Jerusalem. My heart has understood great wisdom and knowledge" (Ecclesiastes 1:16, NKJV).

Those who support the theory that Solomon's pen is responsible for Ecclesiastes, suggest that it was likely written during the latter years of Solomon's life, when he began to sober to the fact of his moral downfall. He finds himself doubting that anything that one might possess has any real and lasting value. He ruminates that, since the rich and poor alike will meet the same fate of death in the end, everything is utterly senseless and meaningless. He wonders whether his wisdom has had any lasting usefulness since, through his depressive lens, life is empty, vain and pointless.

If Solomon is the writer, and I am inclined to believe that he is, then he was in a sorry state of mind when he wrote it. I have known and counseled people who were gripped with paralyzing depression, and a common theme among them is one of hopelessness and despair. They cannot seem to find anything to rejoice and find hope in at all. The depression just sits on them like a heavy blanket. This appears to be Solomon's condition while writing Ecclesiastes. He is *vexed* by everything *under the sun*.

Solomon, however, does not decry wisdom herself, but he does seem to decry what wisdom has wrought through him and others, especially if one loses his focus. As the book begins to wind down, it is apparent that Solomon is starting to find some clarity. It is as if he is starting to see above the clouds with the light of the sun burning through the dark veil that had been on him as a result of his descent into sex-crazed-idol-worship.

If Ecclesiastes were a symphony, most of it would sound dark, cold, dreary and gloomy. However, it does not end on a sour note, nor does it disappoint. In truth, it would be an elaborate composition that takes its listeners on a masterful journey. Solomon, its composer and conductor, starts with the problem, but ends with the solution. He crescendos his opus in a mighty way. It is as if there were brass, woodwinds, strings, symbols, and drums decreeing in unison, harmony and chorus the whole summation and culmination of his experience when he finalizes the piece with the words: "Let us hear the conclusion of the whole matter: **Fear God** and keep His commandments, For this is man's all. For God will bring every work into judgment, Including every secret thing, Whether good or evil" (Ecclesiastes 12:13, 14).

Solomon, near the end of his life, had come full circle. For him, the conclusion and the essence of life itself is bound up in the fact that mankind will be judged by God, and there will be no exception. The secrets of the heart will be revealed and all will be exposed and naked "before Him with whom we have to do." Therefore, according to Solomon, if there is wisdom to be gained, utilized and exercised, let it begin at its foundation and its source: the *fear of God*. The fear of the Lord is wisdom indeed (Luke 2.35; Hebrews 4.13, KJV).

No man had arisen to the heights of wealth, fame, and honor that Solomon had up until that time, and likely very few have attained a similar stature after him. Yet, for Solomon, no material possession gained, no praise from a prelate's lips, no *sexcapade* with the world's premier women, could compare with the truth that he would ultimately stand before his Creator and give a full accounting of his life. This was a pragmatic truth that began to awaken him from his stupor. Every choice, every decision, every hidden motive would be clearly laid out before God.

He knew that the fear of God was the source of all wisdom, and he understood that its natural outworking would be that right choices and decisions would come from it. He concluded that a life lived with a healthy respect for God would lead in all good ways, and everything a person should require, and some things that are desired, would come along with it. He was aware, painfully aware, that when the fear of God leaves so does wisdom, and when wisdom departs nothing good fills the vacuum.

Let us learn King Solomon's Secret, which is to prize the *fear of the Lord*, and through it, let us learn to be wise. We must possess wisdom to guide us through the many challenges that we will regularly face, and we need wisdom to aid in providing solutions to the varied needs of our communities and the people we love. There are people that'll willingly surrender to Christ, the Lord, by witnessing the excellent fruit of our lives.

So, if we desire to be used of God and to be the problem solvers of our world, let us rediscover and live in the fear of God and never let it go. Here is a prayer to help us stay on course or get back on it. Feel free to pray it or write your own. Also, please copy it and share it, should you desire to, with anyone you'd like.

> Father God, through Your precious Son, Jesus, and by the aid of Your gracious Spirit, return to me, in its fullness, the right and proper respect for You in every area of my life: my relationships, my sexuality, my words, my finances and my choices. Let me know and walk in Your fear, O God, and allow me to be a holy example to those around me while I operate in Your wisdom. It is in Jesus' Name I ask and pray, and it is for His glory that I desire You to do this. I believe that I receive what I have prayed even now — amen and amen.

Solomon's Secret in Your Hands

In the pages that follow, we will unpack King Solomon's Secret. As you rediscover and reinvest this great truth into your heart, my prayer is that you will experience what I have been privileged and blessed to find while studying, preaching and writing the subject of this book. Specifically, I found a renewed sense of awe at the grandeur of God, a deeper sense and desire to walk in a way that brings him pleasure, and a deeper yearning to see the people around me come to the saving knowledge of Jesus Christ.

While no person can claim to have the corner on any truth found in the Scriptures, and I do not make that claim with this work, I feel confident that this book will enliven a strong working knowledge of the fear of the Lord into your hearts and minds. You will be able to share King Solomon's Secret with others, in your own words, and I pray that you are inspired to do so.

It is also my hope that, as you read through my personal testimony of how the fear of the Lord chased me down and overwhelmed me until I was saved, you will be inspired to turn to the chapter on the "Seven Secret Steps to Successful Prayer" and begin to pray for those you may have given up hope of ever seeing saved. I was radically transformed from a life of total rebellion to one of complete surrender to the will of God. My wife (she was my girlfriend at the time) discovered the Savior ten days after I did, and her reason for surrendering to Him was that "If God could save him, He could save anybody, and I wanted that God."

I was blessed to be part of an outpouring of God's Spirit that witnessed a youth group go from 35 teens to over 350 in less than six months, and many of them were swept into the Kingdom of God in the same fashion that I was. I was preaching the Gospel within days of finding Christ, and I have been ever since. Within seven months of turning to the Lord, I was preaching in local schools. I believe King Solomon's Secret may be a missing link or key in seeing another Great Awakening sweep over the planet. The fear of God is sorely missing in the church and in our world today, and I hope this book would aid in seeing its return.

You will be amazed to discover that the Apostle Paul, the most dynamic New Testament figure outside of the Lord, was driven, motivated and compelled by King Solomon's Secret.

Abraham, too, the patriarch of Israel and the father of faith to every believer on the planet, past and present, was known to possess the Secret as well, and it drew the commendation of God Almighty during his greatest test. Additionally, King Solomon's Secret drove Abraham's incredible life of intercessory prayer and left us with an indispensable example for us to follow as we pray for those that we love.

Furthermore, Jesus, the fulcrum upon which the Old and New Testament pivots and to Whom every past and present believer must yield their successes and achievements, spoke poignantly and clearly about King Solomon's Secret. He did not mince words, and through it, He even revealed deeper depths of worship as He combated Satan in the wilderness temptation and left every believer a living example on how to intensify their devotion to the Heavenly Father.

I have prayed for every person that holds this book, and I have asked the Lord to reveal Himself in new and living ways. If one person is transformed by this book, then laboring over these pages the last few months has been worth it. May the Holy Spirit guide you and bless you in your reading, and may *King Solomon's*

Secret become your living reality. May you rediscover the wonders of the *fear of the Lord*, in Jesus' Name.

Chapter Two
The Secret That Saved Me

I couldn't sleep. Day and night, rest escaped me, and when I finally did manage to fall asleep, it was only in short intervals. The reason I couldn't sleep was due to being terrified, terrified of not waking up—ever. The thought consumed me, and I began to walk around like a zombie as my every waking moment found me contemplating the prospect of death.

As if the pervasive thoughts of death were not enough, it was compounded with horrifying mental images of dying and going to hell. I began to sense that hell was a very real place, and I knew that I did not want to go there. I had been living an immoral life of promiscuous behavior, along with a steady diet of illicit drugs and alcohol. At the time, I never considered that I would be granted entrance into heaven if I died. I had a supernatural sense that, should I die, hell would be my eternal home, and I could not shake the feeling.

It didn't matter if I was distracted by partying or if I was out with friends. I could not escape a sinking feeling that I was doomed. I imagined a cell in hell where I would be held captive awaiting my final judgement. I thought about the lake of fire and eternal suffering. I did not want to go there, but I knew I deserved to. At the time of my experience, I was 21 years old, and I hadn't darkened the door of a church since the age of 14. Seven years had passed since I had listened to a pastor speak of eternal things. Even when I did go to church, I cannot say that I had heard much about hell prior to my terrifying episode, except at the close of worship services when appeals to be saved were made. I am sure my parents had warned me of it, but I cannot say that I recall them doing so. However, I am certain they were praying for me.

I did not have a strong theological reference point for understanding the realities of eternal separation from God, but the thought of it seemed to sit upon me.

While intoxicated, my heart would race and the sensation of death would become amplified, and frankly I began to think that I might be losing my mind. I begged God for mercy and made copious promises to never again, if He would let me live, use drugs or alcohol, but I was powerless to quit. I always returned to my sin.

After a couple of weeks of torment, I was invited to a bachelor's party on Saturday the 14th of May, 1994.

The party was a typical brouhaha with all the trappings meant to maximize a groom's final hours of singleness. Drink, drugs, strippers and pounding music filled the hall where we enjoyed the revelry. At some point, and I don't know exactly when, my surroundings and my memories of the evening faded into a blur. What I do know about the evening was from people who were present and later shared with me. From what I was told, I had begun to act exceedingly drunk in spite of having not been there very long. I have often wondered if someone had slipped something into one of my drinks, but there is no way to know. Nevertheless, whether from what I had already consumed or from being drugged, I began to act excessively intoxicated and out of sorts.

After a couple hours had passed, some of the guys decided to head to a bar in an adjacent town and asked me to come along. I agreed, but while I was leaving, a close friend of mine asked me to first drop him off at his girlfriend's house, so we jumped into my car and shot out of the parking lot. He had been persistent in wanting me to give him a ride, and I must have grown irritated with his demands, so rather than meet the other guys at the bar, I raced to take him to his girl's place.

I sped along in a drunken attempt to drop him off, and looking back, I was probably rushing in haste so that I could meet the other guys at the club. While driving above the speed limit, I zipped past a few teenagers who were forced to jump out of the way, because I almost hit them. One of the kids in the group told me later that I took a hard right turn up a side street and my front left tire popped sending my car spinning into a tree. My father had been warning me to get the front tires changed for a few weeks, but the fact that I hadn't likely became a major contributing factor in saving my life. It is entirely possible that the spin slowed my car down enough to keep me and my passenger from life threatening injuries.

I do not know how long my car was t-boned against the tree, and I am certain the impact had knocked us both unconscious. Strangely, from the point that I woke up, I have a clear recollection of the rest of that fateful evening.

My buddy was unable to open his door, because it was pinned against the tree, but he managed to squeeze his body through a small opening in the shattered passenger side window. It was his side of the car that was pinned against the tree. As the sound of sirens filled the air, people began to pour from their houses. My friend cried out, "Get out of here! The police are coming!" He began pushing my car from the curb.

My car had stalled, but I managed to get it started, and I proceeded to my house on a completely flat tire and with my headlights out. The damage to my car was significant enough that anyone surveying it would question why the car was on the road in the first place.

Within moments, I was blinded by the lights of a police cruiser. Rather than stop, and I cannot tell you why I didn't, I turned up the street where I lived with my parents and siblings.

I finally stopped in front of my house, and I was immediately asked, from the officer's loudspeaker, to exit my vehicle slowly and lie face down on the ground. Two other police cars arrived as I exited my vehicle, and each officer emerged from their cruisers with their weapons drawn. Sadly, as I was being cuffed and taken to one of the police cars, my father arrived home from his evening shift at the local steel company, and was there, along with my mom and siblings, to witness me being hauled off to the city jail. My dad asked one of the officers why I was being arrested, and the look of anxiety, worry and panic upon my dad's face is something I shall never forget.

People began to line the sidewalks on both sides of the street, and as I was driven away, my eyes locked with my mother and my two younger sisters who were standing close to her. She held both of my sisters close to her hips, their heads nestled under each of her arms, as the three of them cried. I sobered rapidly.

I had rejected God wholesale from the age of 12 until that moment at 21 years and 8 months old. I didn't know that I had, but that is, in fact, what I had done through my life's choices. I had an awareness of Him, yet I lived a godless existence. I fornicated at every turn possible, and I tried many different kinds of drugs while habitually imbibing. I was completely filled with love and lust for self, and I had no intention of changing. However, the thought of dying and going to hell had begun to afflict me intermittently in my early teens and had increased to night and day for about 3 weeks prior to my accident.

I believe this was the catalyst God used to ultimately humble me and save me.

They Have No Fear of God at All

The Apostle Paul, author of a large portion of the Bible's New Testament and an exceptional example of the transformative power of *King Solomon's Secret*, penned these words to the Romans when discussing the lost state of all humanity:

> "As the Scriptures say, 'No one is righteous - not even one. No one is truly wise; no one is seeking God. All have turned away; all have become useless. No one does good, not a single one.' 'Their talk is foul, like the stench from an open grave. Their tongues are filled with lies.' 'Snake venom drips from their lips.' 'Their mouths are full of cursing and bitterness.' 'They rush to commit murder. Destruction and misery always follow them. They don't

know where to find peace.' 'They have no fear of God at all.'" – Romans 3:10-18, NLT

The apostle, like a doctor who takes an honest assessment of the symptoms afflicting his patient, details with precision the universal problem of mankind. He does so through a clear and concise diagnosis. Paul, reasons that the choices, words and manner of living of the lost are corrupt, foul and evil, and he deduces that there is no soul in the world of man that is righteous of his own accord.

He finds, in the condition of man, outside of the saving mercies of God, at least 12 symptoms:

- Unrighteousness
- Foolishness
- Pride
- Rebellion
- Utterly contemptible and useless in the presence of God's holiness
- Not capable of any good at all, especially moral goodness
- Foul in speech and language
- Duplicitous and serpentine-like in word and deed
- Mouths filled with blasphemy, cursing and bitterness
- Murderers of men in heart and mind and deed
- A bent toward destruction and the spread of misery
- Without peace of heart and mind and incapable of providing lasting peace for anyone else

Symptoms merely indicate a root issue, an underlying cause. Paul understood this fact, so after clearly laying out the 12 symptoms, he diagnosis the disease: ***they have no fear of God at all***. The common disease within man that ties sin to his life and rejects repentance in favor of obstinacy is the disease of not possessing *the fear of God*. The King James version of that part of the verses says, "There is no fear of God before their eyes." In other words (Paul is quoting the Old Testament Psalmist in 36:1), the world view of the lost is shaped by and their choices are produced from a lack of reverence and respect for the majesty, power and grandeur of God.

This was exactly my condition: I did not fear God. I did not believe that my sin had separated me from God or that my sin would be judged. I had never taken time to consider that I would be taken to task for having heard the Gospel clearly and still chose to reject it. I rejected my parents counsel, and I rebelled against all that was good and just and true.

Sadly, in conversations with my friends, while under the influence of alcohol, I claimed to love God and believed that I was blessed by Him. Any good thing that happened in my life I attributed to His divine favor and assumed, falsely, that it was an affirmation of my life and choices. The truth was, however, that my life choices actually betrayed me and said otherwise, and I was blinded and could not see who I really was, not until the terror of death and hell struck me sore.

I had moments of clarity over the years, but it was during my three sleepless weeks that I began to contemplate the man I had become and the possibility of my eternal destination. The thought bore down heavy upon me and refused to lift.

I did not know it at the time, but the *fear of God* was manifesting in my life, speaking to me, compelling me, and terrorizing me. Visions of hell and its very real possibility, along with the thought of impending death, consumed me and robbed me of rest. In my tired and depleted state, I probably drank more than I should have that night. Perhaps I was drugged. Whatever the reason for my inebriation, it was only my sorry choices that catapulted and launched me into that tree that evening, nearly stealing me from the Earth. No one and nothing else could be blamed. I am convinced that had I died that evening—had my tire never blown so that I would smash into the tree at full speed—I would have fallen right into the heart of hell itself, never to return and never to emerge. I would live in eternal torment for all ages and for all time.

God Inside of a Police Officer

I sat quietly in the back of the police car, and frankly, I was contemplating the amount of time that would be necessary for my most recent choices to blow over. I knew from previous troubles what my parents' response might be, and I was pretty good at gauging the length of time necessary to move beyond it. I was still filled with pride and selfishness in spite of my car wreck and arrest.

I have observed over my 22 years of continual ministry that negative circumstances cannot entirely turn a person in the right direction, and whatever changes there is in a person's lifestyle, they are usually temporary at best. I am not suggesting that people have not changed based on a life event. I am sure there are exceptions to every rule. But with hands cuffed behind my back, I was proving my theory to be correct. I was already considering an easy exit out of my trouble, and at that moment, I did not even consider changing for the better.

When we arrived at the police station, the officer removed me, still cuffed, from his cruiser. The night was quiet and warm, and the steady breeze off the lake made our lengthy walk to the station more tolerable. I remained quiet as he held my left elbow, insuring that I wouldn't flee and that I wouldn't trip and bust my face open with no hands in front of me to cushion a possible fall. Suddenly, and very unexpectedly, the officer spoke, and his words pierced my pride and my selfishness. As if I were a balloon filled with my worst self, his words acted like a needle that deflated me and emptied me of my pride. I shall never, as long as I live, and I believe long into eternity, forget his admonishment, "Paul? What is wrong with you? Why are you living this way? Man, you have a great father who loves you; why are you doing this to him?"

I melted and my arrogance was crippled. My false-confidence was shattered, and my defense mechanisms were debilitated. Perhaps reading his words 22 years after they were first said does not have the same import as they did upon me that night, but I must emphasize that they were no ordinary words to me. They were graced with heaven. The Almighty stooped down and spoke to me through a police officer. His words were timely and anointed by the Holy Spirit and they held an uncommon power. I was ripe for hearing them, and they pierced me to my soul. However, he did not stop with his admonitions about how I was living and the effect they were having upon my dad. No, he continued and said, "You need Jesus."

You need Jesus.

He said it with tenderness and love, and at that moment, everything within me knew that he was right. I didn't argue and I didn't disagree. In fact, I responded, "I know. I know."

When I affirmed his statement, a humility washed over me. I lowered my head, and I released my pride with those four words. He said nothing else to me, and I was booked into the city jail.

I realized, sometime later, that the three weeks of terror and the prospect of death and hell had set me up for that moment. No, I am not suggesting that God had gotten me drunk, nor am I saying that He nearly killed me to allow me to hear those words. Quite the contrary; He had been trying to save me from that crash. That evening, before my wreck, my mother was mopping her kitchen floor and was suddenly struck with an overwhelming urgency to pray for me, and she fell to her knees in desperation and pleaded with God for my life and for my soul. My dad, while showering prior to leaving the mill, was struck with the same sense of impending disaster for his son. So, I believe with certainty that God did not wish for me to be drunken and hit that tree. However, God was going to speak to me at some moment and at some point, and He sovereignly chose that police officer (thank God for the officer's willing obedience) and that event to do so, and I am eternally grateful that He did.

After being booked, I was escorted up an elevator to spend the night. I had made a couple calls from the common area of the overbooked jail, and angry drunks, drug addicts, and recently arrested violent offenders jeered and scolded me for making my calls while they attempted to sleep. I shouted back, yet they persisted. Foam mats were scattered everywhere on the floor, and I was handed my own, along with a filthy blanket and smelly pillow. Apparently, the eight cells in the pod I was locked in were filled up. I had hoped someone would come get me, but I didn't know who would, and I suspected my parents were inclined to let me sit in jail for the weekend. As I attempted to doze on the four inches of foam while hoping for release, I slipped back into a selfish and pride-filled state of mind. I contemplated ways to talk myself out of my trouble.

After an hour or so of laying on the floor, sleep having escaped me, persistent thoughts of death and hell returned. I began to feel exceedingly agitated and angry. I wished desperately for the thoughts to stop, and I longed to be out of the stink of sweat and urine that was the city jail. I tossed and turned, and I battled incredible feelings of anger and rage toward God. My mind felt like it was about to snap when I heard my name called. Finally, I was being let go—someone had come to pay my bail.

My father's sister had been my deliverer that early morning, and I asked her to drop me off at my girlfriend's house, which was next door to my parents. After a brief few moments of recalling the accident to my girlfriend, I finally drifted off to sleep next to her.

My First Few Steps Toward God

Early the next day, which was a Sunday, I was awakened by my girlfriend's mother, telling me that my dad wanted to see me immediately. I put my shirt on, said a few words to my girlfriend, and headed over to my house. I was prepared for the usual long lecture.

As I sat on the bottom of the stairs in the dining room, I wondered what my dad might say, but he didn't say anything. After sitting in silence for a few more minutes, I went upstairs to wash my face, and I laid down on my parent's bed hoping for a little more rest when they called me to come back down. Again, I sat on the bottom of the stairs when my dad finally spoke, "You have two choices, and I think you know what they are."

That was it, twelve words, and they were the only words he spoke. I waited for him to say more, but he didn't. I looked at the pain in my mother's eyes, and along with my dad's few words, I felt a deepening sense of remorse. The humility I sensed with the police officer returned. I watched my siblings, who were exceptionally younger than myself—my parents did not have more children until I was 12—playing with one another, and I felt that I had been an incredibly poor example. I don't know that I had ever felt that type of conviction prior to that moment.

I made my way back up to my parents' bedroom, plopped back on their bed, and I began to contemplate my dad's words. I knew what he meant, or at least, I thought I knew. He meant that I could move out of the house or I could quit living the way I had been. Conviction upon conviction began to roll over me, and I knew with complete clarity that the only hope of being freed from my sin, the only hope for relief from the terrible prospect of death and hell was found in that officer's words. I knew I needed Jesus.

My mother came upstairs to check on me, and I laid quietly in her room as she pretended to be there to hang clothes. After a few moments of awkward silence, she said, "Honey, you know me and your father only want the best for you, right?"

I knew they did; there could never be any denying her words. I sat silently for what felt like an eternity, but what was likely only seconds, and I fought and attempted to hold back the words that pressed against the back of my mouth and begged to be released and spoken. There was a battle raging on the inside of me, and it was going to be winner take all.

I finally spoke. I gave way to the swell that was my desperate plea for freedom, and my humble cry of submission. "Mom, I don't want to live this way anymore. I want to live for Jesus."

I hadn't even planned to speak in that manner, but that is how my soul responded. Tears rolled from my eyes and face and that of my mother. I found myself broken and feeling the weight of years of rebellion and evil leaving me. Shackles were being unlocked. We hugged and cried for several minutes.

Everything began to be clear for me. My soul found some light, and I knew I didn't want to let it go. In that instant, I was aware that I didn't have to go to hell. It all made sense. *The fear of God was King Solomon's Secret.* It had terrorized me for about three weeks, intermittently throughout the years, and had lead me to that moment in my parent's bedroom. Now it had become the most sublime sweetness to my thoughts and soul.

However, there was still one more thing I needed to do, and I knew it in that moment with my mother.

Chapter Three
The Secret That Hounded Me

Francis Thompson's poem, *The Hound of Heaven*, is an expose of a pursuing God eager to save a sinner, the sinner's rebellion and rejection, and God's willingness to persist even through long years until He, at the end, has conquered the man's heart. It is likely that Thompson's poem is a biographical sketch, and His opening lines speak of the universal condition of all people before surrendering to God: "I fled Him, down the nights and down the days; I fled Him, down the arches of the years; I fled Him, down the labyrinthine ways/Of my own mind; and in the mist of tears."

Over the years, I've heard sermons from various preachers and teachers referencing the *Hound of Heaven*. Not necessarily did the minister quote the poem directly, but often they simply used the term to signify the dogged pursuit God often employed to save a person from destruction. The phrase always bothered me, because it provoked the idea, in my mind, of a hunting dog—a *hound* dog. How could God, I often pondered, the Almighty, be compared to a meager dog?

I have no experience hunting with or without dogs, so I was left with little understanding of the import of the phrase or what the author may have meant when he penned the words that have inspired great Gospel preachers the world over. My ignorance was only exacerbated because of Elvis Presley's famous 1956 #1 hit record, *Hound Dog,* and the opening lines which were emblazoned on my young mind: "You ain't nothin' but a hound dog, Cryin' all the time, You ain't nothin' but a hound dog, Cryin' all the time, Well, you ain't never caught a rabbit, And you ain't no friend of mine."

I could still imagine the black-and-white old footage of Presley and his curled upper lip, his gyrating legs, and his beautifully coifed light-brown hair as he belted out the famous lines. My confusion was understandable. Elvis' hound cried all the time and never caught rabbits, and I'd never seen a hound hunt in my entire life. How could God be considered the *Hound of Heaven*? It wasn't until a friend of mine, who *runs* dogs, shared a couple of insights with me about his hunting dogs that my understanding was somewhat enlightened.

The first thing he told me was that his dogs had the task of ferreting out the game that he was hunting for. Their superior ability to scent the game in question made them necessary to detect the game's location and to excite the game so that he and his fellow hunters could have a clear shot. Next, he pointed out to me that his dogs were relentless and resolved to bringing back his master's kill. The dog never let up until his master was pleased, and his master was only pleased when the prey was in his hand.

It was after listening to his very brief explanation, in laymen's terms, that I realized what God did in my life when bringing me to salvation. He found me where I was and exposed me for who I was, leaving no place for me to hide. He pursued me relentlessly until I was tired and weary from the pursuit, and He never gave up His chase until I had been slain by His love and struck down in His grace. I finally understood: The Hound of Heaven was none other than Jesus, and by means of the Holy Spirit, He employed His chiefest weapon of choice: **the fear of God**.

I have heard often that God is drawing and wooing us by His love. Of course, since God is love, such a statement cannot be false, but it is certainly tainted in our minds. We tend to fancy love as a feeling, much like romantic love or like the warm feelings we may feel from time to time as when we are among our closest companions. However, if it was God's love that nailed Christ to the Cross, and it was, and if it was love that kept Christ there, and it was, then how can we reconcile such a horrible scene, as the brutality in which Christ suffered, with warm fuzzy feelings? The problem lies in our fallen thoughts and not with God. I felt no love whatsoever until I surrendered my life to Christ—totally and completely surrendered—and I had not totally done that in my parent's bedroom. More on that in a moment.

Jesus said that, when the Holy Spirit comes, "he will convict the world of its sin, and of God's righteousness, and of the coming judgement" (John 16:8). Additionally, He made it very plain that no one can come to the Father unless He, Jesus, drew them to Him. It is the work of God's Spirit to bring down conviction for sin. Without the Spirit's aid, men would find themselves perpetually and habitually miserable with no means of understanding their present state or where to find hope for their souls.

There is no reformative power available in men to release the soul from its sin laced condition, even though eager men may try. All of the modern practices of prison systems may help a person leave jail and become a productive citizen of society, but they cannot make him any good to God. Neither can any psychiatric measures heal man in his deepest hurt and help him with his deepest need. Only God can do that.

As long as there has been medical discoveries and medicinal helps, people have begged for their aid. Those that do find a little help are often left disappointed by the often temporary and inconsistent relief they provide. Mankind's quest for permanent relief from his deepest inner conflicts leads many toward the abuse of illegal and illicit drugs. They'd rather bypass a physician's help altogether in their hunt for solace. People everywhere may not even know why they abuse drugs or alcohol. Many, frustrated by the continual inner storms that never quiet, abuse these substances to the point of physical debilitation or death. With each overdose, we are reminded that the deepest yearning of the soul cannot be quenched with the highest highs.

I once ministered to a lady who needed medication to wake up, medication to get through the day free from panic and anxiety, and medication to go to sleep. The poor woman was a walking zombie, and it was tremendously hard to reach her because she was overly medicated. Many people are like this, and it might be that we are medicating a world into oblivion with every attempt to cure them, when in reality, the pain they carry and the psychosis that afflicts them could be remedied through the power of a surrendered life to Christ.

When Paul penned, by the Spirit, that there was "no one righteous—not even one…No one does good, not a single one" (Romans 3:10,12), he was advancing the truth of the universal sin and fallen state of mankind. This is a notion most of us recoil from, for it is hard for us to accept that even when we are at our best, apart from God, we are still damned.

It is difficult for the mind to conceive that the little old retiree at the local retail entry way, who may have never obeyed the Gospel, is eternally condemned. Yet she is. How tragic it is that we cannot or will not fathom that the high school buddy, the one that would drop everything to be by their friend's side in a crisis, is dangling over an eternal chasm, and should they fall in, God forbid, they would be in eternal torment and everlasting torture. But that is what will happen if they never obey the Gospel and trust Christ as their Lord.

Sadly, most of us wish our friends, colleagues and family would know our Savior, yet we feel helpless at times to aid them in seeing the truth. We simply do not know how to assist or what to do. By the time we do work up the courage to invite them along to church, we are repeatedly rebuffed. When they do succumb to our wishes and visit a church service, they don't hear much that would immediately overwhelm them and motivate them in making an instant lifesaving decision to surrender to Christ. There is little to no conviction for their sin.

This is why we must not understate the work of the Holy Spirit in Christ's pursuit of the lost, and it is why we must get thoroughly acquainted and comfortable in understanding His work, not only in our lives after we have received Jesus, but just as importantly, before.

I think it is important that I share how radically I was saved and some of what I was saved from. Though to be honest, I am quite embarrassed by the rebellious life I once lived. However, before I write about it, I need to share the rest of my story from Sunday, May 15, 1994.

Finally Caught

While sitting on my mother's bed after shedding our tears, my friend's face flashed across my mind. I had not seen in several months. He had shared his faith with me, and I had an overwhelming sense that I was to call him. Additionally, I instantaneously remembered his name though I had not even considered him since the last time I saw him. We had met at the local community college where we shared a choir class together. I had been enrolled in the music program because I was a guitar player, had a band that I played with, and thought that the additional training might help me before I headed out to California to pursue my dream of going to the Guitar Institute.

All at once, I recalled that he told me that he was in the phone book should I need to reach him day or night. I found a phone book (these were the days before smart phones and dial-up internet service), and I decided to call him right at that moment to see if he was attending the evening service at his church. I knew the church well, because it was the one I refused to go to from the age of fourteen. My mother was a former member of that church and several of my family still were active members.

I dialed my friend's house, and to my surprise, he answered. He was shocked to hear that it was me calling, and he seemed to be very excited about the fact I had. I asked if he was attending the evening service, and he told me he was and that he'd love for me up to go along with him. He picked me up about 30 minutes prior to the start of the service, and I immediately told him that I desired to get *saved*. In my mind, I had come to believe that to be truly *saved*, one had to go to an altar at a church and say *the sinner's prayer*. I was innocent, without much knowledge, and the Lord was so gracious toward my ignorance.

There is no doubt now that the Holy Spirit had been directly involved in recalling to me my friend's face, his name, and how to find him. He was vigorously at work on behalf of the Beloved *Hound of Heaven* to bring me to the place of total surrender.

When we arrived in the auditorium of the church, I was stunned to see many of my family members. Sure, I expected to see my mother's sister and possibly one more, but several of my cousins were there—cousins I had done some pretty despicable things with. I started to get cold feet. I knew there was going to be an *altar call* (an altar call usually takes place at the end of a service where sinners or backsliders are invited to come forward to meet the pastor or with a prayer worker for the intent of accepting Jesus into one's heart and life), there had been one at every single service I ever attended, every weekend from the ages of 12 to 14. I had resisted every one of them. With each rejection, I felt my heart grow colder and harder. Sitting there watching my family, I decided that there were too many familiar faces for me to go forward at the end of the night's service.

I'd love to say that the service was a fire and brimstone message that would cause the worst offender to run to the front begging for forgiveness, but it wasn't. In fact, it was a dedication service for young girls who were committing themselves to sexual purity before God. I was nervous the entire time, and since one of my young female cousins was in the ceremony, it became apparent to me why so much of my family was present. I also believe it was a divine set up. Jesus was going to see if I was ready to proclaim my commitment to Him in the presence of those who knew the life I had been leading. Would I be too embarrassed of Him and still too filled with pride? Would I insist on doing things on my terms or on His?

Although there wasn't any preaching, I was still under the heavy hand of conviction the entire ceremony. The Holy Spirit was working upon me in spite of the order of the service. True to form, at the close of the meeting, the senior pastor gave a 5-minute Gospel message, and it was potent. He spoke of eternal salvation and damnation in crisp and clear terms, and he made it plain that if a person died without choosing to follow Christ, and without being born-again, they would be forever lost. It was as if he had been in my head by the things he said, yet when the time came to raise my hand and move to the front, I resisted. I had invisible cinder blocks on my feet and they were strapped to the floor.

My friend reminded me that I had come to get saved, yet I protested. I asked him if we could just pray in his car to which he said no. I had to move when the Spirit was prompting and not, nor never, on my terms. My pride took a hit, and I am so grateful it did. He asked me to go forward again and I declined a second time. The preacher was still making an earnest appeal.

For a third time, my friend pleaded with me to go up to the altar, but before I answered, he wanted to show me something, and I agreed. He pulled a sheet of paper from his Bible that had been dated about 3 weeks prior, and my name was there at the top. He said to me, "Paul, you see your name on this paper? Look at the date. We have not seen each other in several months, but the Lord told me a couple of weeks ago to fast and pray for you, and I have been, since this date, and then you called me today. Paul, this is the day you have to be saved. You have to go up there, man. This is the moment you have to go forward. Come on, and I will go with you."

With his remarks, the cinder blocks broke form my feet, the straps loosed, and I practically ran to the front to meet a prayer worker. I repeated a prayer with the worker as I sobbed, and with every deep groan, years of rebellion were shattered from my life. I had acknowledged Christ before many, and I was finally humbled enough to at last answer an altar call in the very place I had resisted so many of them.

The most remarkable aspect of what took place that night, immediately after I concluded praying and weeping, was a tremendous sense of overwhelming peace and joy. The weight of my sin left me, and I felt a tangible absence of it. Strangely, I did not know that it was a heavy yoke upon me until after it became clear to me that it was gone. I smiled from ear to ear, and I could not stop. The *fear of God* had done its job, and Jesus had conquered His child.

Fully Free by the Power of Solomon's Secret

Beginning at the age of twelve, I began to reject God for a life of rampant sin. Having children myself, it is hard even now for me to consider that a twelve year old would start living as I had. I smoked marijuana and drank alcohol for the first time and began to do so with increased regularity. Within a couple of years, I was sneaking out of my parents' home, climbing down my balcony, and running through alleyways to meet friends so that we can go to bars and play pool. Often we would be served beer without being asked our ages. The establishments we frequented were not places where kids should have been allowed, and looking back, I feel a sense of anger that no adult ever asked our ages or told us to leave.

In the summer I turned sixteen, I smoked more pot than I had in the previous years combined. Additionally, I drank beer or some form of alcohol nearly every summer day and almost daily well into the school year. My grades suffered, and I began to skip classes. As well, I tried other advance types of illicit drugs (pot is truly a gateway drug), and I began to fornicate habitually. I maintained a steady diet of sin from which I did not want relief, but around the close of my sixteenth year, I began to have occasional confrontations with the *fear of God*. For the first time, I began to dislike the life I was living, but I felt hopeless and helpless to stop.

Finally, at the age of seventeen, and after my dad had been sharing the Gospel with me, I went to my bedroom and asked Christ if He would enter my heart. For about thirty days I lived a changed life, but I never changed my friends, nor did I attend church or hang out with other Christians. I tried to tell my friends that I had found God, but they shrugged it off as a fad. When I went back to my former ways after the thirty days, I felt different. There was a darkness and a heightened awareness of a sinister force inside of me. I became violent. My friends and I began to create problems and ruckuses wherever we went. We were hell bent and bent on hell, and Satan had me fully. If any spirits had gone out of me in my bedroom that day…well, they came back, and they came home with uglier friends. I was fast tracking to hell.

Most of my friends sold drugs, and they spent money on me and with me. I barely worked, and I scarcely kept jobs. What money I had I used up on debauchery. I spent the summer after graduation working at an amusement park, which should have been named Sodom and Gomorrah Amusement Park, because every type of sin was available, and I dove head first right in. I looked for as many women as I could find, and I never left a bar alone. I was snared and I knew it, and then the *fear of the Lord* started up again. It increased incrementally, but it became a regular occurrence, and around this time, I began to have frequent run-ins with the law.

My life was unravelling.

I was arrested once and I was also investigated for another crime while working at the amusement park, but there was not enough evidence to bring charges, and eventually I was fired after kicking the door in of one of my roommates I disliked. I did it just to see if he and his buddies wanted to have a good tussle, but they didn't comply. I left the amusement park only to continue my godless living in the city. I pressed on with my reckless behavior right up until the day I was marvelously saved.

Here is the most miraculous and amazing part of the story, and why I believe the *fear of God* must return to our lives, cities and our churches: I was completely and utterly set free of every vice, habit, wicked-yearning, longing, perversion and sin. I am not overstating what took place, and before God, I would not lie or exaggerate. I was loosed from every acute and chronic perversion and rebellion, along with the deep desire to do those things as well. I did not leave that church on May 15th and try to do better, like I had when I was seventeen. No, I left that place and I *was* better.

Jesus had made me better by liberating me and by putting His Holy Spirit within me.

What was even more incredible, and had I not been the person living it I might not believe it, was that I rarely had a temptation to go back to my former ways. Sure, from time to time, I felt some sort of external dark power attempting to beckon me back—Jesus said we would have that problem occasionally—but it was no longer inside of me, driving me and pushing me toward sin and sinfulness. Yes, corrupt memories tried to plague me, because I had lived in a despicable manner for so very long, but again, they did not possess the same force and strength over me. Jesus had set me free—hallelujah!

Every one that knew me recognized that something had happened, and I have been tempted to believe that God had some sort of special deliverance just for me. However, that would be inaccurate at least and prideful at best. Truthfully, and I learned years after, our region was under a sovereign outpouring of God's Spirit that was activated by men and women who had positioned themselves to see God bless the region.

Let me explain. Years after I began my journey with Christ, I examined, through observation, the experiences of others who had begun their journeys with Christ at roughly the same time I had. The similarities were remarkable. To be certain, I did not conduct a scientific survey, though I wished I had, but had formulated my findings through, as I said, observation and discussion. What I found was that many reported an awful sense of divine justice lingering over their lives, and others shared how they were immediately liberated from long held vices just as I had been. They reported similar one-hundred-and-eighty-degree-turn-arounds.

King Solomon said in Proverbs 16:6, "And by the fear of the Lord *one* departs from evil." I have considered that verse to imply that if a man *feared the Lord*, then he would be inclined to depart from evil. In other words, he would do so of his own accord, over time, and after consideration of his life choices. However, I have come to discover that the *fear of God* itself is the force that liberates, because I was a recipient of its instantaneous, liberating power. The *fear of God* drove me to Calvary's Cross!

It is imperative that the Christian understand that God desires to see people freed in similar fashion and with frequency and regularity. I have been in full-time Christian ministry for many years and have friends in the same vocation, and very few report the kind of conversion experience that I and many others had. In fact, it is this problem that lead me to examine my own conversion, the exceptional nature of it, and the details surrounding it. It is also the reason I felt prompted to write this book. I believe the *fear of God* might be the missing piece of the puzzle for so many pastors and churches.

Of course, it is not that people aren't finding Christ in our churches, but many that do struggle through terrible habits and sin patterns that beset them for years. This is not God's best, and it should not be ours either.

I began this chapter talking about the *Hound of Heaven* and His work upon my life, but an honest assessment, a survey of sorts, of what was happening behind the scenes, which led to so many similar stories of incredible deliverance and life changes, is necessary. When we understand the many aspects of the *fear of God* and how it was released upon a region, we will find renewed zeal and vigor. We will be encouraged with a new zest for seeing our loved ones, colleagues and neighbors saved in the same manner as I and others had been.

The question begs to be asked: How do we see our homes, communities, and workplaces come under a similar sense of divine justice, the *fear of God*, and is there anything we can do to help it? The answer may surprise you. Please turn to the next chapter to find out more.

Chapter Four
Solomon's Secret Resting on a Region

"Paul would you pray for my friend? He'd like to receive the baptism of the Holy Spirit." It was a Wednesday night teen gathering in December 1994, and one of the high schoolers was asking me to assist him in seeing that his friend could come into a fuller experience with God. Now, depending on your doctrinal persuasion, especially about the giving and receiving of the Holy Spirit, gifts of the Spirit, and whether or not you think people who believe such things are completely mad, you might be tempted to end your reading here, but please do not. Allow me to share what God did in a youth group that went from 35 kids to over 350, in steady attendance, in less than six months.

I promise I am not going to try and sell you on praying in tongues or any other gifts of the Spirit, because my goal for this book isn't to argue theology. However, I must share what took place after my conversion, how it came about, and how we can experience God moving sovereignly most of the time, and not just occasionally, or only in far off places. If there are people in your world whom you want to see delivered as I was and find freedom as I did, then please keep reading.

We had just concluded a two-hour youth service filled with a rockin' band and powerful preaching. I wasn't even in Christ eight full months, and I was already heading up a team of altar workers that were responsible for praying at the close of each Wednesday night service for the varied needs of the teens that would come forward. Additionally, I held regular prayer gatherings with some of my team, and we prayed for thirty minutes prior to the start of every youth service, along with other teenagers and adult workers.

That youth group was blessed with an incredible youth pastor that loved the kids, invested in them, and released others to assist him and his wife in facilitating the outpouring of God's Spirit. He believed in holy living, preached with incredible passion, and the church he was on staff with loved and adored him. I was honored to be a small part of what God was up to. It was he that recognized a leadership gift in me and empowered me to serve alongside of him. In fact, he was the prayer counselor I had prayed with at the altar the night I was miraculously saved eight months prior.

I was busy counseling another person and I could not immediately fulfill the request of the young man that asked me to pray for his friend, but he asked me again about two minutes later. I assured him I would, but he needed to wait until I finished with the person I was tied up with. Kids milled about and talked, others received prayer, while some knelt and prayed quietly. Music played softly overhead. Again, the young man tapped me on my shoulder and begged, "Brother Paul, would you please pray for my friend? He wants to be filled with the Holy Spirit."

Again, I asked him to wait. Ever persisting, he asked me once more, and I again declined. In retrospect, I have come to believe that this was the sovereign hand of God leading me to turn him down time and again because of what was about to happen.

What happened next is nothing short of supernatural. I felt a physical force swirl about from behind me in the a-frame chapel where we held the youth services, sweep around the inside of the building, and blow up the front of my body. It felt like wind, though I am unsure if anyone else felt it. At the precise moment I felt the wind run up my body, and while the young man I was counseling was in mid-sentence, my whole person was turned around independent of my will, and I pointed a finger at the young man that I was being appealed to pray for, and I yelled loudly and boldly, "You foul demon spirit, you come out of him in the name of Jesus!"

I wish I could tell you I had consciously said these words, but I cannot. I do not recollect ever having said them prior to that moment, and it is highly unlikely that under different circumstances I would have uttered them. At least, not of my own accord. When I made my spirited declaration to him and pointed my finger at him, he flew back as if someone had pushed him down, and he fell flat on his backside. Instantly, I positioned myself over his body, and with two other teens by my side, I yelled again without knowing what I was really saying, "Come out of him, you devil. Come out in the name of Jesus."

He growled loudly and turned over on his stomach. He began to claw at the floor in a mad and desperate attempt to flee. Foam bubbled out from his mouth while he gurgled, growled and screamed loudly. In fact, the many people still left in the room stopped to witness the tumult near the altar. I told someone to pick up his limp body as I heard a voice say to me, "He isn't free yet. Continue to rebuke the devil."

It was not an audible voice, but it was as clear as if it had been. I continued to rebuke the spirit that was obviously putting up a fight.

We had to pick him up several times, and I heard the same instruction each time. Suddenly, and all at once, he became lifeless as if sleeping. Drenched in sweat, he lay on the floor in a state of utter peace and contentment. I had seen this same boy earlier in the night, in the last row of the auditorium, and noticed an angry and bitter scowl on his face as he sat unresponsive to the service. I also remembered that as he had responded to the appeal to follow Christ, he had the same angry visage, but now, as he lay upon the floor, a smile sat upon his face. He glowed.

Later, this teenager, who I eventually mentored and who later went off to Bible college and in time became a pastor, told me that while he was in that youth service he had heard a voice telling him to leave and run out of the place. He recalled how he listened to angry words in his head telling him that all of the worshipers were fake and the Gospel was not real. He said he wanted to sprint from his chair never to return. He had determined that he would harm himself or harm others, but that another force would not let him leave the building. That inner tug warned him that if he were to die, he would die without Christ and suffer forever for it.

He shared how he had begun to embrace various forms of occultism and dark arts and how he had a growing fascination with ancient oriental practices. However, as a child, he had seen in a dream a man being consumed by fire while never being fully destroyed, and the man gnashed his teeth and screamed in total torment. He awoke from the dream yelling at the top of his lungs and weeping uncontrollably. His mother ran to his side but was unable to console him.

That early vision had continued to work upon him right up to the moment he was sitting in the back of that auditorium. The reality of hell's destruction and torment would not leave his thoughts. He had wanted to reject God, but something would not let him. He had wanted to dive completely into the dark powers he had started to experiment with, yet something held him back from being fully immersed. That something was the *fear of God*, and it kept him from being destroyed by darkness.

Guest ministry teams would come to that youth group and each one of them would testify the same way, saying, "We thought God was sending us here to bring you guys something, but it was us that needed something, and we have been more blessed by being here than we have blessed you all."

It was an incredible demonstration of the Spirit's outpouring, and it should not be uncommon in the church, and it should be prevalent in our homes.

It was not unusual for the youth pastor to get phone calls from high school officials begging him to "tame these Christian kids" because they were excessively evangelizing the schools. Some teachers admitted that the students were among their very best and among the most respectful, but they were overly zealous in wanting their friends to know Christ. A student was reprimanded for standing atop a table to declare the Gospel. One of the principles called the church to request that the kids not *lay hands* on fellow students on school property. Some students were uncomfortable, understandably so, seeing other kids lying on the ground crying and praying in *weird* languages.

Teens from the youth group organized after school clubs geared to seeing other kids come to Christ, and they were wildly successful. Two of the leaders of such clubs, in two different high schools, invited me to come preach to their friends, and one of the events was complete with a full band. There were over fifty kids present with many surrendering their lives to Jesus. I was only saved about seven months when I went and preached to the students, and I've been preaching ever since.

I'm certain some of my story may appear exaggerated and perhaps a touch too wild, but I hope what ultimately comes through, more than anything else, is that many lives were transformed. Yes, we were young, and indeed, we had plenty of zeal with little knowledge, but God blessed our passion, honored our abundant prayers, and souls were added to the Kingdom.

I am also aware that since some readers may have never experienced anything remotely near what I and many did that they may be inclined to reject it as emotionalism. They might even be fair with such an assessment, but having lived through it—myself being a person who is typically and initially skeptical of such claims—what I have shared is completely true, accurate, and is actually under exaggerated. Others may be thinking, "What on earth has any of this to do with the fear of God?" These are valid concerns and questions.

In fact, we were not seeking for these kinds of demonstrations and manifestations when they were thrust upon us. Rather, we were thrust into them. There was a tangible sense of divine justice that sat upon our region and people were swept into the Kingdom of God. These kinds of experiences have not been uncommon throughout history, and there is evidence of similar things right in the Bible.

It would be unfair for me not to mention the fact that there were other churches in our city that were having similar experiences. I am certain that if Christian scholars had recorded and analyzed what had taken place in our region, they would have classified it as a classic example of revival. These were the days of the Toronto Blessing and, a couple of years later, the great Brownsville outpouring, so it is not unreasonable to think that there were other pockets of revival happening around the world that were hardly noticed by outside observers.

In each of the places mentioned above, along with some of the churches in our city, intense and earnest prayer for God to save the lost and pour out His Spirit preceded the great visitations. The senior pastor of the church that had the incredible youth program that I mentioned above, about two years before I was set free, fasted for an entire year on vegetables and water for his church and his city to be mightily blessed by the Lord. He organized prayer initiatives, held convocations, and initiated around the clock prayer before it was fashionable.

I'd love to say that I was part of the preparation for what I experienced in my conversion and what we partook of in the youth group, but that would be a lie. I had nothing—zero—to do with it. I am simply honored and blessed that he and his team of hungry believers gave themselves to prayer so that I and many others would be swept into the Kingdom of God.

My aunt had given my name to her prayer group, my parents were in continuous prayer for me, and my friend from community college had been fasting for me as well. My salvation and deliverance, though a sovereign act of God, included the earnest will and desires of people, prompted by the Spirit, who were unwilling to let me go to hell.

Sure, after I was saved, we began to pray in earnest for God to do greater, but it is only because we saw the example of people like the senior pastor, youth pastor, my parents, friend, and other leaders of the church. These were people intent on seeing God's glory manifested, and God did not disappoint.

Peter, the Fear of God, and 3,000 People

The New Testament book of Acts records that three thousand people were struck with a sense of impending disaster to their souls, their hearts being pierced by a message delivered from an uneducated former fisherman, and they begged to know what they needed to do to be saved. Peter, just after the great outpouring and giving of the Holy Spirit known as the Day of Pentecost, preached a clear and concise Gospel message, and the impression it had on many of the listeners was stunning:

> "Now when they heard *this*, they were cut to the heart, and said to Peter and the rest of the apostles, 'Men *and* brethren, what shall we do?'" - Acts 2:37, NKJV

Peter answered their question by graciously imploring them to repent. Next, he commanded them to evidence their desire to turn to Christ and follow him through water baptism. As I shared above, 3,000 people came to God that day. In fairness, the scriptural record does not say that the fear of God came upon them, but by the fact that they had a sense of desperation to be saved we can assume with some accuracy that that is what happened. Why else would they demand to know what they should do?

These people that heard Peter's message were cut to the heart and then begged to learn how they too might be saved. When was the last time there was a church service where people begged the preacher to be saved and not the other way around? All too often, people are told by well-meaning preachers that they ought to give Jesus a try. Sinners are encouraged to give the Savior of mankind a test run? However, Peter had a different message altogether when he warned them to "be saved from this perverse generation" (Acts 2:40).

I would not argue against making visitors and church members comfortable, and indeed, there is a balance preachers must strike in tone and tenor, but there was something potent in Peter's words that we might learn from. These were words streaming hot and heavily from the lips of a man that was newly transformed, and his radical conversion should not be understated. He went from a fisherman to a fisher of men just as Jesus had promised.

Prior to Pentecost, in Acts 2:1-13, and just before Jesus' trial, death, burial and resurrection, Peter denied Him, not once, but three times. He then went back to his fishing business, forgetting that he had left it to apprentice with Jesus as a fisher of men. Jesus, after conquering the grave, mercifully forgave Peter and welcomed him back into the apostolic ministry. Jesus then commanded Peter and the other disciples to wait in Jerusalem for the giving of the Holy Spirit. Peter, along with about one-hundred and twenty others, continued in prayer, and God honored their obedience. He poured His Spirit upon them.

Suddenly, the man who ran back to his former life was now preaching a message with words that were like arrows dipped in the blood of Jesus and set on fire by the Holy Spirit. He hit his listeners dead center in their hearts.

What happened next seems to confirm what we had experienced as well and at least verifies that our visitation was not a contradiction of Scripture:

> "Then those who gladly received his words were baptized; and that day about three thousand souls were added *to them*. And they continued steadfastly in the apostle's doctrine and fellowship, in the breaking of bread, and in prayers. Then **fear came upon every soul, and many signs and wonders were done through the apostles**. Now all who believed **were together and had all things in common**." - Acts 2:41-44, emphasis added

It is remarkable that the fear of God came upon everyone. If two, or maybe three, people who happened to be more pious than everyone else had been the only ones reporting that they were encountering the fear of God, then we might be justified in overlooking the use of the phrase in the text. Since you're probably like me in that you find great importance in every word and term used in the Bible, then the fact that "fear" came upon "every soul" becomes profoundly important. It bespeaks of a widespread supernatural phenomenon. It is not speaking of a few overly religious people who were living in a way that was not commonplace. Instead, every man, woman and child had a profound reaction to the fear of God. I am reminded of what happened during the season in our town when so many people reported similar experiences before and after trusting Christ. The fear of God was upon us just as it was then in the book of Acts.

Additionally, Acts 2 tells us that extraordinary demonstrations of God's power through the apostles' hands, called signs and wonders, accompanied the fear of God. At the expense of sounding a tad presumptuous and a smidgen arrogant, I have to say that we too experienced, along with the fear of God, incredible demonstrations of God's power.

It is not untypical for God to do things within a set mode or operation that He has predesigned. I am very aware that God is not bound or relegated by patterns, but even nature teaches us that when God sets something in order, say, for example, the air currents, He rarely deviates from His original designs and plans. Occasionally, and we pray infrequently, wind related events occur such as tornadic activity that upsets the beautiful balance and patterns of nature. These events are not the norm. Sadly, in our modern Christian era, we have come to expect the exception to be the rule and the norm to be the exception to the rule. God sees things different and will wait for us to become desperate enough for us to align our eyes with His.

Lastly, and probably the most important outworking of the fear of God, was that the believers "were together and had all things in common." Christ followers are called to be abundantly generous to one another, habitually hang out with each other, and treat each other with love, care and dignity. However, and sadly, we don't hear too many testimonies from outside observers of Christians in particular in cities or neighborhoods that sound similar to the one in Acts 2. The fear of God melted away from them all divisions along every line and caused them to esteem each other better than they did themselves. They wanted to be "together" and found every opportunity to do so.

When the fear of God is upon a people, it is not likely that they will be inclined to gossip and slander one another. During the mighty outpouring that I experienced, we found ourselves together as well. We prayed together, we ate together, and we stayed late at one another's residences because we were compelled to by something greater than ourselves.

I have spoken with many pastors, and some of them would love to have small group ministry in their congregations, but they find it nearly impossible to pull off. Some have told me that they have tried different approaches and styles only to be met with tepid results over and over again. Still others have given up completely while maintaining that modern Christians are just too selfish for small groups to be successful. It is not modernity that is to be blamed for the selfishness of any person, including Christians, because people are naturally selfish and have, since the fall of man, always been. Therefore, excusing the failure of small group ministry as being the direct result of selfish people is likely more of a cop-out than anything else.

Churches must simultaneously grow larger and smaller, but small groups should not be just another optional program that churches offer attendees. Rather, small groups—some churches call them life groups or cell groups—should be the natural and organic outgrowth of normal Christianity. Perhaps what we've called selfishness is nothing more than the modern Christian being spiritually asleep, possessed by apathy, and lacking deep reverence for God. I don't remember anyone, during the outpouring I was part of, ever instructing us to get together or to be generous to one another. No, it was a normal function of our Christian experience.

Church programs have two major problems hard wired into them. They are expensive to maintain and they must be managed by experts. Jesus never assigned professionally trained people to advance the Kingdom of God. I am not suggesting that training is unnecessary for Christian service, God forbid, but one need not have a college education, as great as college is, to lead a small group or to oversee small group leaders. Additionally, they do not need to be paid staff either. Sure some paid staff will be necessary at different intervals of a church's growth, but many churches run top heavy and fat just like many national governments do.

When the fear of God was given to the early church in Acts 2, it does not say that they immediately started a food pantry, back-pack give away, singles ministry, or youth group. None of those things are necessarily bad, and we certainly need them, and churches do an amazing job doing them, but those things do not advance the faith or transform lives as effectively as an outpouring of the fear of God will, which produces habitual togetherness and generosity.

Christianity has always done best from a grass roots level, and it seems to fair better when it runs lean. I know of one church that has a 40,000 plus membership base and growing with 3,500 small groups, and their staff is a measly 400 full-timers. I have examined this church and interviewed key staff personally. They have the smallest, per capita, staff to member ratio in the United States of America. If, for some unforeseen reason like persecution, their church had to close their doors, the work of God would still go forward because their small groups are wildly effective. Since they have been in existence, which is, at the time of this writing, about fifteen years, they have seen crime drop in some of the most crime ridden neighborhoods of their city, due, in part, to their emphasis on consistent prayer, and placing small groups in these neighborhoods. They are habitually together, and it is changing the region. I can attest to the fact that the presence of God hangs over the city and that people were being saved in mass in several of the services at various locations that I attended.

The Fear of God Versus Fright

When I was a child, there was a popular horror movie whose main character would kill his victims in their dreams when, and if, they fell asleep. It was the first movie in the horror genre that I had ever been exposed to. One of the key lines of the nightmarish fright movie was "Don't fall asleep."

My pals and I were riveted and consequently terrified by the scarred villain and his razor sharp finger extensions used to slaughter his prey. We dreaded going to sleep after watching the movie. The writers, producers, actors and directors had done their jobs well. We were thoroughly fear-filled. A common mistake that we make is thinking that the fear of God has to do with fright and *feeling* afraid.

Whereas the feelings of fear that are provoked by a horror movie are designed to cause the viewer to fawn, cower and cringe away in fear, the fear of God is not designed that way. Rather, the fear of God has little to do with fright, being afraid or cowering in terror, but more to do with provoking an awe inspiring view of God that compels us to worship and regard His magnificence in a healthy manner.

It helps ward off deviations from truth and holiness like idol worship and apostasy. Additionally, the fear of God compels us to view a fellow believer and the world around us with profound accuracy, seeing through different lenses that are much closer to how God sees us and sees those who are still rejecting Him. We end up loving our Christian brothers and sisters and longing to witness to the lost without allowing resentment, judgment and a bitter attitude to skew our perception of them.

It's true that while a person remains outside of Christ, the fear of God may provoke feelings of incredible terror and gloom, especially at the horrendous prospect of hell, but even that is geared to cause the sinner to eventually repent and receive the Lord's gracious free gift of salvation and deliverance. My own experience has taught me—as stated in chapter two—that what was once a terrorizing force upon my thoughts and soul was turned into the most sublime sweetness after I was saved. I found my Father's love and He found me through the fear of God, and I ran into His waiting and open arms.

In the Bible, God's people are often and repeatedly referred to as sheep. I am no sheepherder, but studying sheep and sheep herding has become a mild fascination for me, and what I have discovered is that sheep have an overt tendency to stray. Some, in fact, make consistent attempts at breaking free of the shepherd's boundary lines in order to wander freely. It makes sense then that God considers His people as sheep, especially since so many of them ride the fence lines of life, looking for the proverbial greener pastures.

I am a father of ten children, five girls and five boys, and I have had plenty of experience with my little ones attempting to wander off into places they ought not be. I have been pressed to discipline them in a way that doesn't harm them further, but at the same time, provoking enough respect in them for me to not try and venture off again. It isn't that my ego needs to be fed by my children's unquestionable submission. It is that I love them so deeply and desire their continual protection from that which could possibly harm them. Provoking temporary tears in them for their missteps will save me and them a multitude of tears later.

A shepherd, whose book I was studying, stated that the safest place for sheep was with within eyeshot of the shepherd so that he could, if need be, drive off any of the many predators that have a taste for sheep flesh. He said that the sheep he usually lost were the very ones that were habitually filled with wanderlust and which never seemed to trust his care for them. In order to protect them from wandering and eventual endangerment, he would take his shepherd's rod, which had been carved from a hard wood and had a rounded ball at the top of it, and he would launch it like a javelin from great distances at his straying sheep in an effort to startle them enough to send them back into the fold. He used fear to protect them.

God's methods and thoughts are exceedingly beyond our natural comprehension, and we struggle at various times to understand Him, especially when we mistakenly process His methods through our limited insight. He is apt to launch His rod of protection and discipline at us when we too find ourselves at a distance from where He desires us to be. There are biblical examples of Him using incredible and somewhat troubling means to keep His people on track. We do well to accept the biblical record as it is, without trying to explain what may not necessarily be easily explained. He is God, the Almighty, and only Sovereign, and if we are humble and honest, we will easily admit that we will never really articulate in infinitesimal terms what is eternally infinite.

Considering the judgement that befell Pharaoh and the Egyptians, the Apostle Paul mused at both God's severity and His kindness. In essence, Paul by revelation of the Spirit, explained that God is perfectly perfect in His balanced nature. He will never be too severe, yet He is not exclusively kind as some have supposed. Much of what is preached today emphasizes God's kindness without the mention of His severity toward sin, sinners and the habitually rebellious. It would be right for us to understand that when God is being severe He is still being kind (Romans 11:22, NLT).

In the chapter that follows, we will investigate an example of God's severity among the early church. We will attempt to see what we might learn from it as it relates to King Solomon's Secret—the fear of God—and how we could apply what we learn to our lives today. We will not necessarily try to answer the *whys* as much as the *whats* of the episode. What we can gain in learning from the judgement and death of a husband and wife who lied about their offering amount is of greater value to us than trying to decipher *why* God allowed such a thing to transpire.

With this in mind, please turn to the next chapter.

— Paul Anthony González —

Chapter Five
Startling Encounters of a Secret Kind

Imagine that you are in a Sunday morning public church gathering. The pastor, in characteristic fashion, rises to the pulpit after the song service to receive the tithes and offerings. After a few words, he invites a singer to lead the church in a *special* song picked for the moment. After the singer finishes, the pastor again ascends the platform for a few more words before he welcomes the parishioners to come forward to bring their financial gifts. As the crowd, one by one, drops their money into the available offering baskets, the pastor stops one of the members, and over the public address system, asks, "Brother Talbot, is this the entire offering you promised to bring the Lord?"

Somewhat caught off guard by the query, Brother Talbot assures his pastor that it is the full amount he and his wife, Sister Talbot, had dedicated to the Lord that very morning. However, what Brother Talbot had failed to tell his pastor is that, while on his way to church, he had some misgivings about the amount he had earlier decided upon and had changed his mind. Brother Talbot felt that his tithe was too large and believed he should keep some of it. He wasn't altogether sure what the church was doing with all of the money that had been coming into the coffers, so he reckoned he ought to keep it and manage it for God, himself.

The pastor, under the inspiration of the Holy Spirit, instantly realizes that Brother Talbot was trying to pull a fast-one on him, and so looking him square in the eyes, he says, "Brother Talbot, why would you lie to the Holy Spirit, and let Satan fill your heart? You do know that you've lied to God?"

Brother Talbot, visibly shaken, tries with no avail to respond, "Why I..." and while attempting to get out his excuse, he drops over dead. The pastor then beckons for some of the teens from the youth ministry to come over and haul Brother Talbot's body outside and bury it in the parish cemetery.

Shortly after the young men took Brother Talbot's body outside, Sister Talbot, who had been running late that morning came rushing in to the service. Noticing Sister Talbot rushing in, the pastor calls for her to come forward as well, and says, "Sister Talbot, is the offering in this envelope the full amount that you and your husband committed to bring to the Lord? This envelope that I now hold in my hands that possesses both of your names?"

After examining the envelope, she cautiously answers the pastor, but not before surveying the room to look for her husband. She assumes he must be in the restroom, and she briefly recalls the phone conversation she and her husband had on his way to church. The phone call wherein they discussed keeping some of their tithes to go out and have a nice dinner later that evening.

"Why yes, pastor. Yes, it is the full amount."

"Sister Talbot," says the pastor, "do you see those young men standing there? They are going to carry your dead body out of this building in the same way they carried your lying husband's body out just prior to your arrival. Ma'am, it is not wise to lie to

God and tempt the Holy Spirit. You and your husband could have easily kept what you wanted without ever dedicating it in the first place."

Upon hearing those words, Sister Talbot, also, dies right at the front of the auditorium just as her husband had. The same young men take her lifeless body to the church cemetery to bury it alongside Brother Talbot. It is a very troubling morning at your church that day, and everyone, including yourself, has come under a sense of wonderment and awe. The fear of God is present in the church.

How would you respond to that kind of a display on a day usually designed for celebration and mirth? Would you want to invite your friends to a church like that? Probably not. Would you think twice before lying or cheating or swindling a fellow believer? Would you reconsider private gossip or an attempt at tearing your church in half with a church split? Would you send your pastor an angry email every time you didn't understand his decisions and directions for the church? Would you scrutinize every sermon, complain about music volume, or remark about the style of songs that were chosen for the service at the most recent gathering? Probably not.

Now, if you're familiar with the Bible, you are likely well aware that my fictional account, albeit very exaggerated fictional account, already happened in Acts chapter 5. If you did not, then please allow me to acquaint you with the verses that tell the story:

> "But a certain man named Ananias, with Sapphira his wife, sold a possession. And he kept back part of the proceeds, his wife also being aware of it, and brought a

certain part and laid it at the apostles' feet. But Peter said, "Ananias, why has Satan filled your heart to lie to the Holy Spirit and keep back part of the price of the land for yourself? While it remained, was it not your own? And after it was sold, was it not in your own control? Why have you conceived this thing in your heart? You have not lied to men but to God." Then Ananias, hearing these words, fell down and breathed his last. So great fear came upon all those who heard these things. And the young men arose and wrapped him up, carried him out, and buried him. Now it was about three hours later when his wife came in, not knowing what had happened. And Peter answered her, "Tell me whether you sold the land for so much?" She said, "Yes, for so much." Then Peter said to her, "How is it that you have agreed together to test the Spirit of the Lord? Look, the feet of those who have buried your husband are at the door, and they will carry you out." Then immediately she fell down at his feet and breathed her last. And the young men came in and found her dead, and carrying her out, buried her by her husband." – Acts 5:1-10

Over the years, I have heard this story preached by different ministers, and I have never been fully satisfied that any of them has done the tragedy much justice. I won't try to explain away what happened to this man and his wife, because I don't fully understand it. Neither will I argue in favor of this kind of dramatic judgement happening in our day. Of course, I believe that we should cry out for God's mercy, and if you are like me, you have been a recipient of His abounding forgiveness time and again.

At the same time, I do not think it wise to explain these events as a once-in-history occurrence from which God has repented and Who now promises to be nicer to us. All too often, in our attempt to get people to love and want our God, we end up sanitizing and ridding Him of (at least in the eyes of those we are trying to reach) His glorious majesty and resplendence. We may be sincere in wanting Him to be more palatable to a modern age, but that is not our job. Because of our desperation for our friends, family and colleagues to know and desire Him, we attempt to explain away biblical narratives like this. We do not need to help God be *anything*. He is Who He will be, and He isn't going to adjust Himself to fit our contemporary conceptions and marketing practices.

Rather than rewriting biblical history, we should read the passages with an earnest and sincere heart that is filled with wonder at the greatness of our Heavenly Father. We should take pause for reflection and to be sure that the motives of our lives are in good stead.

I am unsure of all the reasons why God allowed this couple to drop over dead for lying about their financial pledge in the presence of an audience, which included the Apostle Peter, yet the Bible does provide needed light on the subject, and the immediate succeeding five verses offer some helpful guidance:

> "So great fear came upon all of the church and upon all who heard these things. And through the hands of the apostles many signs and wonders were done among the people. And they were all with one accord in Solomon's Porch. Yet none dare join them, but the people esteemed them highly. And believer's were increasingly added to the Lord, multitudes of both men and women, so that they brought sick out into the streets and laid *them* on beds and couches, that at least the shadow of Peter passing might fall on them." – Acts 5:11-15

The Startling Encounter's Aftereffect

The first effect that the death of Ananias and Sapphira had on the church, and consequently everyone else that heard about it, was that the *fear of God* was poured out on them. While it is not hard to believe that people might be afraid if they heard such a story, we must note that this was not a fear that might be explained or described as fright (please look at the end of the last chapter, under the subheading *Fear Vs. Fright*, for a further discussion on the difference between fear and fright). Rather, it was a supernatural reverence for God. It was the kind of fear that righted the courses of men's lives; the same kind of divine respect for God that delivered me, and others, and redirected our life choices. We did not try to change ourselves, because we could not, but it was done by God working mightily in us through His Spirit. He released upon us, through the earnest prayers of His people, a sense of impending divine justice, and it changed our decrepit practices into godly living.

The Message Translation presents a more accurate understanding of the original Greek used in the rendering of verse 11: "By this time the whole church and, in fact, everyone who heard these things had a healthy respect for God. They knew God was not to be trifled with."

"They knew God was not to be trifled with."

It is sad to note that we are living in an era when, in many nations of the earth, all manner of lewdness and immorality are, not only practiced, but normalized and legitimized. It would be one thing for the church to look out on the world, in its unsaved condition, and observe these things, but it is quite another thing to see practices that once made people blush being received and encouraged right in pulpits that formerly condemned them. Of course, we were once part of that darkness. We also understand that our calling, as Christ followers, is to reach the world with His light and life and extend grace and mercy. However, Christians may find themselves participants in things the Bible condemns through incessant silence.

Ungodly living is welcomed in many denominations and churches, and any argument or opposition against wickedness is often met with hostility, accusations of bullying, judgmental-ism and legalism. God is being trifled with, and the fear of God has left the church. **When the fear of God leaves the church, the church leaves God**, and when the church leaves God, the culture-at-large follows.

When the fear of God rests on a local assembly of believers, it resides on the families of that group of people, which in-turn, affects neighborhoods and beyond. If Christians don't have a "healthy respect" for God, while disregarding any appeal to abandon evil and sin, then how can the culture be preserved? It cannot be.

Trifling with God is a dangerous practice, and even though we haven't seen the kinds of displays that the early church witnessed, we must not assume that we never will. How long will God be patient? I pray that He will be more patient than He already has been, but I am not certain that He can indefinitely allow godlessness to run rampant among His people.

There is a vast difference between a person who is struggling with sin-challenges and tendencies and a person who is practicing, promoting and endorsing sin as a biblically sanctioned lifestyle. We are in an era where sinful behaviors are encouraged and preached as being acceptable to God, and He will not remain still forever. The fear of God must return to our churches, and if it doesn't, I believe that it may come at a hefty price.

The next thing that transpired as a result of the lying couple's death was that "signs and wonders" were "done by the apostles' hands." I believe the reason for this is that God has an impeccable and remarkable way of balancing His severity with His kindness. These precious believers had just witnessed an incredible demonstration of what happens when sin meets God's holiness dead-on, but oh, how gracious of Him to meet their profound needs with displays of His goodness and power.

It is important to God that people come to know Him as a *God of love.* Constant demonstrations of correction and discipline would have people believe that He is anything but good and long suffering. He, no doubt, wanted the outsiders who had heard of His chastisement upon this couple to know that He cares and that He was willing to heal them of their afflictions. We have been privy to God's underserved grace and kindness in *our* own lives, and we should continually rejoice in it, yet His mighty acts toward us should result in making us all the more willing to reject sin whenever it rears its ugly head.

It should be that His lovely nature compels us to get rid of all things that are an offense to Him and His magnificent holiness—and not a motivation to abuse His kindness. Humans are bent on seeing how far they might push His patience, and possess an overt tendency to stray. I make it a constant prayer of mine that He keep me and that He deliver me and those I love from the inclination of our flesh to rebel. He has never failed my humble appeal, always bringing me back when I have found myself wandering.

More than anything, He longs to see people come to Him and be saved from eternal destruction and misery. A person's worst day on this earth will not compare to the flames of torment that await those who partner with Satan in his ongoing rebellion with the God of heaven.

I buried a sister fourteen years my junior. She was a gift from God to me, and I had a unique and special friendship and bond with her. Because of our age difference, I was a father figure to her in many ways, and my children adored her and her infectious, vivacious personality. The pain of seeing her lifeless body on a hospital gurney will never, in this lifetime, escape me. My other sister's fainting upon hearing the news, my mother's shock, and my father's wails are burned into my memory. It was the worst time of my adult life and ministry, and it threw me into a pit of despair that I saw no way out of.

I laid on the carpet of my bedroom closet in a puddle of tears for days, yet lovingly and patiently, Jesus came to me and lifted me, little by little, out of my despondency. A few times during that season, it saddens me to admit, I thought I might snap and leave the Lord altogether. It isn't that I wanted to, but the temptation to do so seemed heightened. In my weakened state and depleted condition, Satan and his demons upped their attacks. I wished for death on more than one occasion. The sensation of an invisible vice pressed upon my skull, and I thought my brain might explode from the agony of my sister's early and unanticipated departure at the age of 21.

But there was my Master, by my side, and He sweetly and tenderly healed my wounds and gave care to my broken-inward-parts. Five weeks before she would leave this planet, she returned to Christ. She recommitted her life to Him like she did when she was a child, and she wept her way back into the Kingdom of God at my kitchen table. It was my birthday—though I doubt she knew it—and it was the joy of her faith in Christ, along with the expectation of an eventual reunion with her, that sustained me through my lowest moments and darkest days.

It was a dreadfully painful season of my life. Two-and-half-years after her passing, I suffered through being awakened every night for three straight weeks in a cold sweat, shaking, trembling and groaning in terrible agony. As horrifying as all of it was, it will not compare to one second of the torment that awaits hell's residents.

Every tear I cried won't equate to the shrieks, groans and wails of the damned. My cries were heard, and the Lord carried me and comforted me, but there will be no comfort for any person in hell for all of eternity. This is why we must cry out to God for His fear to be seen now so departed souls won't meet His holy terror later.

Being uncomfortable with the deaths of Ananias and Sapphira is a normal and acceptable reaction. However, as hard as it may be for us to understand God's ways, it is the last outworking of their unfortunate demise which affords us some clarity: "Believer's were increasingly added to the Lord, multitudes of both men and women."

Heaven was populated and hell plundered because Ananias and his wife were struck down. Their deaths released the fear of God. The fear of God resulted in signs and wonders, and people were saved in droves.

God is interested in souls and it does not please Him to send people to hell. We might be uncomfortable with God's methodology, but our present discomfort will mean little in the light of the glory that is coming later. What awaits us after this life cannot be articulated well enough for us to grasp and lay hold of its reality, yet God can, by His Spirit, reveal those things to us. Inside of each child of God is a yearning to be with their beloved Father in heaven. We may not understand the yearning or translate it properly, but it is present within each Christian heart. It is this longing within us that drives us to want to see those we love and care for in His eternal glory with us. Without a confession in Christ, they will not be. We must begin our earnest and heart-felt appeals to heaven to pull-no-punches in saving our loved ones. We must beseech God to remove all stops with a no-holds-barred-hold-nothing-back effort to save our families and friends, which includes a mighty release of the fear of God back upon our local churches.

In the next chapter, we look at a remarkable New Testament figure whose life was altered when he encountered the fear of God. So dramatic was his transformation that the world has never been the same. He led soul winning efforts and church planting campaigns that have been unparalleled by a single person since. Additionally, he left a written legacy that billions upon the earth look to for guidance, for deeper Christian practices, and for understanding. His primary motivation for his intense efforts and for the legacy that he left will likely shock you, and it may not be what you think.

I believe that we are about to embark on the greatest day for Christian evangelism efforts the world has ever known or seen. I suspect that more churches will be planted over the next 10 to 20 years than in all of the years of Christianity combined. I am also convinced that it will be due to radical conversions and the core motivator like the one we will review in the next chapter.

Chapter Six
The Secret Motivator

What drives you? What compels you, and why do you do what you do? For some, the answer is an easy one, yet for others, it may be that they have never stopped to consider the question. However, everyone is motivated by something. For example, during my younger years, my mother was the chief motivator to get me off to school. I hated my formative scholastic experiences, so I unintentionally honed my mother's motivational skills, which she would use with great tact and precision in dealing with my younger siblings that came after me. As we age, we find ourselves doing various things for a wide range of reasons, but there is not one thing that we do that is not being motivated by something or someone.

Star crossed lovers are moved by passion to travel great distances to visit their beloved, while some athletes find the impetus to achieve great success because they were told by the so-called experts that they were too small or too slow to make it on an elite field. Others, who grew up in a perfectionist environment and never having sensed the acceptance of a parent, have an insatiable drive to achieve notoriety and prestige because they long for the praise and affirmation that was absent from them in their formative years. Whether we know it or not, there is something or someone driving every one of us to do the things we do.

The Apostle Paul was no different, and in his second epistle to the believers in Corinth, he shared what his greatest motivator was for becoming the most prolific writer of the New Testament in addition to being, what many believe, the single greatest evangelist and church planter:

> "Knowing, therefore, the terror of the Lord, we persuade men." - 2 Corinthians 5:11, NKJV

The breadth of Paul's impact on the church age and western civilization in general cannot be understated. The churches that were planted by Paul and his team in many parts of the west (western Turkey, Greece/Macedonia, and Italy) went on to become extraordinarily influential to the western church and ultimately Western culture and society as whole. Ethics, mores, political constructs, and judicial systems of the West were all fashioned, in some part, by the Pauline church plants, writings, and Christians that had been influenced by them. There is little doubt that Paul was a nation shifter and world impactor, and his motivation? ***The terror of the Lord.***

In order to understand Paul's use of the phrase and what he claims was his foremost catalyst for persuading men to be saved, we must consider his pre-conversion life in conjunction with his upbringing and early life's experiences. As well, we cannot overlook his dramatic encounter with the Lord on a road to Damascus, Syria.

Paul, who's Jewish birth name was Saul, was born in 5 AD in a city called Tarsus in the Roman province of Cilicia—today would be the southern coast of Turkey. He was a Roman citizen by birthright. He hailed from the Israelite tribe of Benjamin—the youngest of the twelve sons of the Jewish patriarch Jacob. He was probably named after the First King of Israel, King Saul, who was himself a Benjamite and stood head and shoulders above all of his contemporaries. However, unlike his namesake, historians tell us Paul was not at all tall, and his little stature may have been due to a sickness early in life. His Roman name was Paulus (He would have been given a Roman name and a Hebrew name), and it meant *little* or *small*. He likely made up in personality and bravado what he lacked in height.

Between the ages of ten and fifteen, Paul was admitted entrance to the prestigious school of Gamaliel in Jerusalem to study the Law of Moses and become a religious leader of the group known as Pharisees. It was Gamaliel, a senior leader of the Sanhedrin (the Jewish Supreme Court), who in Acts chapter 5 cautioned his judicial colleagues against taking steps to kill the apostles for preaching the Gospel. Gamaliel's ability to influence the court was due, in part, to the high respect he had among the people for being a regarded teacher of the Law of Moses and for being the grandson of the famed Hillel, the former president of the Sanhedrin. Some biblical scholars also believe that Gamaliel's father was Simeon, mentioned in Luke 2, who held Jesus as an infant and prophesied over Him.

The Pharisees, one of three dominant Jewish sects during the time of Jesus, found themselves often the derision of our Lord who called them the offspring of snakes and children of Satan. This was largely due to their incessant scrutinizing and systematizing of every aspect of the law, while being morally lax themselves. While the Sadducees, one of the other sects mentioned in the

Gospels and Acts, were *freethinkers*, the Pharisees were *formalists*, or what might be called fundamentalists.

The Pharisees held that the Law of Moses was divided into two sacred transmissions: The written law and the oral law. Sadly, the oral traditions took on greater value and was held in higher esteem than the Word of God given to Moses on Sinai. Their misguided respect for oral traditions over the inspired written Torah was the reason Jesus, during His Sermon on the Mount, attacked their hypocritical false righteousness when He said, "You have heard that it was said to those of old" (Matthew 5:33).

When Jesus said, "You have heard that ***it was said to those of old***," He was subtly leveling an attack against the religious leader's dependency on the oral Torah rather than the inspired Word of God written by Moses and others. Jesus personally held the written Word of God in the highest regard as evidenced by his interaction with Satan in Matthew 4 and Luke 4, respectively.

At some point—and the Bible lends little insight as to how—Paul became radicalized. Gamaliel was liberal and progressive in his Judaism, at least as far as the new Christian sect was concerned, but not Paul. He made it his personal mission to wreak havoc upon the church. He issued threats, called for the deaths and arrests of believers, and even obtained warrants so that he could personally detain and incarcerate any Christian that he found engaged in a public or private expression of their faith. Paul was possessed with defending his brand of Judaism against Christianity, and he was zealous to do anything he could to stop it (Acts 9:1-2).

In addition to his religious extremism, there is ample evidence to support that Paul was greatly influenced by the Stoic philosophers of his day. Self-denial and personal discipline were part of Paul's missionary work after his conversion, so it is not unreasonable to think Paul's philosophical worldview before meeting Jesus was impacted by Stoicism. As well, Paul's regular use of the concept of a human "conscience" in his writings would have no doubt come from men like Athenodorus, a famous resident of Paul's hometown of Tarsus, and who once said, "Every man's conscience is his god."

The idea of a *conscience* within man is nowhere to be found in the Old Testament, and it is probable that Paul was calling upon Stoic influences when he wrote the words: "Who show the work of the law written in their hearts, their conscience also bearing witness, and between themselves their thoughts accusing or else excusing them" (Romans 2:15).

When considering Paul's extreme Judaism, combined with a Stoic influenced philosophy of self-denial, we can extract the driving force behind his hate-filled persecution of Christians. He likely resented the fact that he was working very hard to obtain a righteous position before God, while the Jewish Christians were claiming that Jesus had died to save *them* from their sins to satisfy the justice of God. This was anathema to Paul.

The emerging Christian rhetoric was an affront to everything he held dear and had invested his life in learning. For Paul, pleasing God was a merit-based proposition, something that must be earned and deserved. Paul had rigorously denied himself creature comforts. Also, he lived an untarnished legalistic life so as to be seen holy in God's sight. He was not going to allow some new Jewish-offshoot to fill all of Israel with perversity about a man who supposedly had risen from the dead to freely give them what, as he saw it, could only be earned through incredible force of will in keeping with Jewish traditions.

We are first introduced to Paul at the close of the seventh chapter of Acts while he was lending his full consent and support at the stoning of Stephen, the first Christian Martyr. Paul thought it his duty to keep the garments of Stephen's murderers so that their throwing mobility would not be restrained by their outer cloaks. Stephen's martyrdom coincided with an outbreak of rampant aggression against the early church, and it was the first time in the church's young history that persecution became widespread.

In 34 AD, two years after the tragic death of Stephen, Paul was still engaged in an aggressive campaign against the church. He went as far as asking for "letters" and a specially assigned envoy to capture and arrest Christians. Permission was granted:

> "Then Saul, still breathing threats and murder against the disciples of the Lord, went to the high priest and asked letters from him to the synagogues of Damascus, so that if he found any who were of the Way, whether men or women, he might bring them bound to Jerusalem." - Acts 9:1-2

"The Way," was an early title given to the church, and while we are uncertain as to the reason why Paul was heading north from Jerusalem to Damascus, we do know that he wasn't going to waste his trip. Paul, ever the ambitious opportunist, took full advantage of his rise in the Pharisaical ranks, and requested special permission to harass believers. However, it would be a trip he would not, could not, ever forget.

As Paul neared Damascus he was overwhelmed by a light brighter than the noon-day sun, and he fell to the ground. Some historians have suggested that Paul was knocked off of a horse, but we are never told that in any of Paul's personal testimonies about the fateful event. It is possible that the phrase, "knocked off your high horse," came from this misunderstanding of the text.

Whether he was on a horse or not, we do know he was stricken to the ground by a blinding light, and he immediately heard a voice saying to him, "Saul, Saul, why are you persecuting me?"

And he said, "Who are you Lord?"

Then the Lord said, "I am Jesus, Whom you are persecuting. It is hard for you to kick against the goads" (Acts 9:3-5).

Most of us are unfamiliar with the phrase "to kick against the goads," but it was a common expression among the Greek and Latin speaking cultures of Paul's day, and he would have understood its usage. When a beast of burden, such as an ox, stubbornly refused to do its duties and farm chores, it was *goaded* by its master in an effort to get it to correspond. There were times, however, when the animal would not respond to the goad and would instead kick back at the prod; the result was always greater injury and pain for the animal.

Jesus was conveying to Paul that He had been poking his conscience for an extended period of time, but he remained noncompliant. His abstinence provoked an aggressive response from the Lord. Jesus had been goading him toward the truth, but he allowed his nationalist pride, love for religious traditions, and lust for career advancement to fuel his hatred and to cloud his judgement. He had to be stopped.

It is compelling that Jesus did not say to Paul, "I am Jesus, and *you are persecuting my people*." Instead, Jesus said to him, "***I am Jesus, Whom you are persecuting***." In the Old Testament, God referred to the Jews as "His people." In the New Testament, God's people are called the "Body of Christ." As far as God is concerned, violence against a Christian is violence against His Son. We, who have trusted in the Lord Jesus Christ, are His Body, and we are the children of God.

When God Asks Questions

When Adam rebelled against God in the Garden of Eden and hid himself away from His presence, God called out to him saying, "Where are you" (Genesis 3:9)?

When Jacob wrestled with Jehovah, he was asked by Him, "What is your name" (Genesis 32:27)?

God could not be God if He did not possess omniscience. He knows everything. When He asked the questions of Adam and Jacob, He already knew the answers. Not only did God know the answer to the questions He posed to these two men, but both, Adam and Jacob, knew the answers as well.

For example, someone might say to another person, "Can't you do anything right?" The question, just like God's question, is a figure of speech called a *rhetorical question*. In the above example, the question was meant to make an insinuation about the person's abilities and not to enquire about their aptitude.

God was making a statement to Adam and Jacob.

Adam answered, "I heard Your voice in the garden, and I was afraid because I was naked; and I hid myself."

Jacob simply replied, "Jacob."

Theirs were simple answers, but full of confession, humility and honesty. There was no need for long drawn out analysis and observations. God knows what *motivates* our *motivations* and what is the *driving-force* behind what *drives* us. A person is usually lying when their answers to personal questions are overly sophisticated and complex. In the presence of the One Whose very essence provokes clear admission, there is no preparation needed prior to answering. In the presence of truth, we are completely disposed; we cannot help but to be simple in our response and truthful with our reply.

God's use of the rhetorical question is always intended to spark a conversation or to provoke a confession. In an instant, under God's spotlight, the interrogated must come to grips with the choices and decisions that brought on their present reality. For Adam, it was for him to come into full view of the weight of his sin, rebellion, and his present nakedness. For Jacob, the question was intended for him to acknowledge the man he had become in light of his birth name—*a supplanter*. To supplant is to overthrow. Jacob had supplanted his brother Esau out of his birthright along with the blessing of their father Isaac (Genesis 3, ch.25 & ch.27).

In each instance, Adam and Jacob are given something after their confession. Adam was given insight into God's future sacrifice of His Son and a temporary stay of his guilt through the death of an innocent victim. He was covered in animal skin. Jacob was given a new name to release a new identity. He became Israel, *The Prince That Prevailed with God.*

Through His indescribable love, God is moved to give the humbled what they could have never provided for themselves. It was a supreme act of grace. Something was needed, and something was given, independent of their ability to obtain it for themselves.

When the Lord asked Saul (Paul) why he was persecuting Him, He already knew the answer. We cannot know the instantaneous personal interaction Paul had with Christ, but we do know that under the spotlight of the divine interrogation room Paul was undone. Every cell of his small frame cried out in response to the rhetorical question. Paul does not audibly respond with excuses and blame-shifting. For it is impossible to do so in such a moment, but that does not imply that there was no response.

A dear friend of mine, a man not given to over-reaction or exaggeration, shared with me a startling vision that he once had. His voice trembled while he retold the story of the encounter, and he barely held back from breaking into tears. He was brought before the Judgement Seat of the Almighty. Positioned on the floor of the heavenly court room, his head slunk down in fear, he rested upon one knee in what he described as "the presence of total purity and holiness."

He told me that a Voice, the Voice of God, surrounded him from every direction and that it filled every space and gap around him. How he understood this fact, he said, "was supernatural."

There was no void when God spoke; no empty space where the vibration of His words could not and did not fill. His Voice came from the top, the front, the sides and the back, and everywhere in between. His Voice had layers of indescribable tones and pitches, but all harmonious and in-concert. The language was foreign to him. However, out of his inner man—his spirit—he responded as did every single fiber of his being. It was as if, he shared with me, he responded down to his molecular level. Only capable of telling the truth, he was overwhelmed by the need to admit what he was before the Lord. There wasn't a place in his soul or spirit where the Lord was not present. Hiding information was futile; he was laid bare.

Paul's answer to the Lord was as simple and plain as Adam's and Jacob's, but it must not be overlooked: "Who are You, Lord?"

His reply was as rhetorical as the Lord's question to him. For in that instant, he knew exactly Who it was that spoke to him and had caused him to fall upon the ground, blinded and trembling with fear. It was his first confession of the lordship of Jesus, and it was his first step out of the clutches of darkness into the light of truth. Paul wrote later, many years after this encounter, that confessing Jesus as Lord is a necessary step toward ultimate eternal salvation, and this experience is how he learned it.

Notice that there was no need to say another thing to the Lord. He did not bother the Lord with sundry questions about the legitimacy of the experience he was in the throes of, nor did he need Jesus to confirm or prove Who He was. Paul was ready to do whatever was necessary to serve the Master in total surrender.

Quaking and astonished, Paul said, "Lord, what do you want me to do?"

With that question, his motivations shifted. In an instant, a future missionary, writer and church planter was born. Instead of punishment and punitive damages owed, Paul found grace, and He was given his destiny while discovering the purpose for which he was born. No longer was Paul driven by selfishness or the thirst for status. He would be forever compelled by **"*the terror of the Lord*."**

The study and preaching of the Gospel became the sole focus of his life, and he would eventually die a martyr defending it. Threatened constantly, he lived a harrowing adventure for the Lord's glory. He was a brave little man. All told, his ministry career extended the space of 20 to 25 years, but who could truly measure the full impact of his life upon the world for generations who came after him?

To say that he was compelled to preach the Gospel is a profound understatement. Paul was possessed by the Jesus that he had met on his way to imprison Christians, and the compulsion, and drive, to tell His story owned him from that point forward and never subsided. He would never relent, and it was, in part, due to a firmly held conviction that God had commissioned him to the task of persuading others from before his birth.

While writing to the Corinthians, he pronounced a "woe" upon himself. He did so in case he ever made the grave error of neglecting to proclaim Jesus' message. Since, from an ancient Middle Eastern perspective, a *woe* is the pronouncement of a curse, Paul was in effect saying that he would rather be cursed than to deny his mission to live and work for the One he once vehemently persecuted (Galatians 1:15; 1Corinthians 9:16).

The Kingdom and Its Power

On the Damascus road, Paul had met the Lord and felt His power. It was a power so great that it left him astonished, trembling and blinded.

I was an electrician's apprentice for a couple of years. Once, while working inside of a very large, industrial sized control panel, I made the mistake of handling the 440 volt *hot* leads without cutting the power. The end of the exposed line touched the wall of the metal panel, and it sparked and blew the power, nearly blinding me in the process. Because it was dark inside the panel, the intensely-bright flash caused me to lose my vision for about the space of two minutes or longer. I was taken to the hospital for treatment and was prescribed a strong salve to apply to my eyes. For about three days, a greenish spot persisted in my line of sight, along with the feeling that my eyes had a sand-like substance in them.

The light that engulfed Paul immediately seared his eyes, and he remained blind for three whole days. Had it not been for a supernatural healing, he would have remained without sight for the rest of his life. When he was healed, a *scale-like* material peeled and fell from his eyes. A traditional Christian belief suggests that Paul had eye problems for the rest of his life, because he mentioned that the Galatians cared so deeply for him that they "would have plucked out [their] own eyes and given them to [him]" (Acts 9:18; Galatians 4:15).

— *Paul Anthony González* —

We all imagine Jesus in uniquely personal ways. It is exciting to think about what it must have been like to be with Him and to watch Him while He walked the earth. He was tender and inviting toward children, loving and stern with His disciples, and direct and harsh with religious hypocrites. At the last Passover meal that He spent with His team, John rested His head on His chest. His nature was surely warm and welcoming.

While we are encouraged to think about the Lord in this way, we must not pigeonhole Him into the three-and-a-half years He evangelized Israel. It is true that Jesus' nature cannot change, but it is equally true that His majesty was veiled during His initial earthly campaign. If we are going to fully know and experience Him, then it is important that we see Him through the lens of what has been written about Him, not only while He walked the earth, but after His resurrection and ascension. His future earthly campaign will look significantly different than His first run.

On one occasion, before His crucifixion, Jesus took three of His disciples (Peter, James and John) up to a secluded mountain and peeled back his flesh-mantle and unleashed His full glory. He warned them not to speak of the event until after His resurrection, because the full revelation of His wonderful presence was for a future time. The experience was more than they could contain. Jesus' face was the brightness of the sun in its full strength; His clothes glowed with a whiteness clearer than if they had been bleached ten thousand-times over. They were shocked and left in a state of awe, so much so, that they fell down upon their knees with their faces to the ground. They were greatly afraid for the *fear of the Lord* had come upon them, and it was nearly identical in nature to Paul's conversion encounter (Matthew 17:1-9).

Prior to taking the men up to the mountain, Jesus had stated that they would get to "see the Kingdom of God" presented with power. They faced-off with the glorified Savior, saw His resplendence, and were marked by the moment for the rest of their lives. Like Paul, they could not walk down from that mountain the same men that walked up. We must not overlook the critical component, according to Jesus, that the fear of God, or as Paul describes it, "the terror of the Lord," has an important part in God's Kingdom.

The Terror of the Lord?

One might call ***the terror of the Lord*** the twin brother of ***the fear of God***, and while some more recent English translations rightly translate *fear* in place of *terror*, it is important to note that *the terror of the Lord* was a concept present in the Old Testament.

There are two noteworthy examples.

In the first example, Jacob was forced to leave a settlement in a city of Canaan called Shechem, because two of his sons, Levi and Simeon, killed all the men of the place. The slaughter was provoked when their sister Dinah had her virginity taken by the regional leader's son. She was unmarried. Sex outside of the bonds of marriage may be as common and acceptable today as sex within marriage, but it was considered a deplorable offense among the people of that time. If a woman had her virginity *violated*, it was akin to rape (Genesis 34).

Shechem, the leader's son who slept with Dinah, desired to make things right and marry Jacob's daughter. Levi and Simeon agreed to it and suggested that all the males of the city be circumcised, and Shechem convinced the men of the city to comply. On the third day, while the men were recovering from their circumcisions, Simeon and Levi came boldly into the city and killed all the men in cold blood, plundered all of their possessions, and took their livestock, along with the women and children.

Jacob, incensed, sternly rebuked his two sons, and feared that his entire clan would be wiped out in retaliation by the other regional tribes. God, aware of Jacob's worries, told him to return to Bethel, the place where Jacob had his first personal encounter with the Lord many years prior. Jacob, after cheating his brother Esau out of His birthright and blessing, fled in fear of his life at the behest of his mother Rebecca. This was long before he was married and before he had children of his own (Genesis 35).

Jacob was aware of the significance of God's directive, because at Jacob's first meeting with God at Bethel, God had confirmed the covenant He had made with his grandfather Abraham and his father Isaac. Jacob would, according to Jehovah, be third in line to inherit God's unique promises to the Jews. At Bethel, God promised to protect him, keep him safe, guaranteed that he would return home from Syria in peace, and that his descendants would be given all the land of Canaan (Genesis 28:10-19).

Additionally, Jacob made a vow to make Jehovah his God and to give Him the tenth part of everything he possessed as long as He would uphold His end of the agreement. God always fulfills His Word. God showed up to remind him, right out the middle of his troubles in Shechem, that He was going to fulfill His promise to guard and protect Jacob and his house. Jacob knew he too would need to uphold his end of the covenant (Genesis 28:20-22).

To prepare his family for the journey back to Bethel (the House of God), he commanded them to perform a ritualistic cleansing. It consisted of changing their clothes, bathing, and surrendering every idol (along with the good luck charms) they had accumulated in Syria. In this way, he was aligning his family for worship so that they could be reintroduced to his God. Jacob realized that his family had become too familiar with the godless customs and manners of the communities in which he had dwelt. He was having a personal, moral and spiritual crisis. Perhaps he blamed himself for the actions of his sons, and we may never know, but he was ready to reacquaint himself and his clan with the Living God (Genesis 35:1-5).

Immediately after Jacob's family obeyed him and purified themselves—their purification was a type of repentance—the Bible records a fascinating outcome:

> "And they journeyed, and **the terror of God** was upon the cities that were all around them, and they did not pursue the sons of Jacob." – Genesis 35:5, emphasis added

The *New Living Translation* of the same verse says, "As they set out, a terror from God spread over the people in all the towns of that area, so no one attacked Jacob's family." Jacob's sons had sinned by personally exacting vengeance on the men of Shechem. Their motives may have been just, but their actions were not. Yet, God, in spite of their sin, saw fit to release His holy *terror* upon all of the towns that surrounded Jacob and his family so that no one would be able to harm them no matter how determined they may have been.

Nearly thirty years had transpired between Jacob's first and second visit to Bethel. Bethel was the place where, in a vision, Jacob saw a ladder stretched from the earth into the heavens, a ladder that angelic hosts traversed and where God stood atop when He made decrees concerning Jacob's destiny. The relevance of Bethel in the life of Jacob and consequently the whole nation of Israel must be underscored, because it was there that God made a significant investment into His future plan for the redemption of Israel and the world. **The terror of the Lord** would see to it that nothing, or any person, could or would stop it (Genesis 28:10-22; 34 & 35:1-15).

About 450 years after God placed his *terror (fear)* upon the towns surrounding Jacob, we find God placing it a second time to paralyze the enemies of His chosen people. After Israel's exodus from Egypt, they wandered, because of their rebelliousness, in the wilderness areas surrounding the Promised Land. Canaan was God's land in the first place, and it was His to give to whomever He chose, and He chose the descendants of Abraham, Isaac and Jacob (Genesis 12:1-3).

Forty years after fulfilling, renewing and refreshing his vow to God at Bethel, Jacob moved his very large clan to Egypt to be near his long-lost son Joseph. Because he had been betrayed by his brothers, Joseph ended up as a slave in Egypt, but he eventually rose to second in command of the entire empire. Lied to by his sons, Jacob thought Joseph had been killed by a wild animal, so he was anxious to go see his son. Jacob's initial plans were to simply visit for a short while, but Joseph convinced him to remain and wait out the remaining years of a severe famine that was afflicting the entire North African region and the Middle East. Jacob complied.

Joseph convinced Pharaoh to give his kingdom's entire sheepherding enterprise into the care of his father and brothers, and they were given prime real-estate in Goshen to set up their base of operations. Sadly, due to the incredible comfort and provisions they enjoyed at the hands of Joseph and Pharaoh, their temporary stay turned into a permanent one (Genesis 37-50).

Long after the deaths of Jacob, Joseph and his brothers, the Egyptian populace and king grew tired of the people of Israel, so they enslaved them. God raised up a deliverer named Moses, and through a series of ten dramatic plagues, Israel was delivered out of bondage. Nevertheless, after walking on dry ground through the Red Sea, watching the Egyptian's elite charioteers be swallowed by the returning walls of water, and being given the Holy Law written by the finger of God, they were still seduced into murmuring, grumbling and complaining. Jehovah gave them many chances to change their doubtful and fear-driven ways, but each time, they reverted back to their dither-ridden state of mind. Eventually, everyone twenty years and above was sentenced to wander in the wilderness over a forty-year span until they died— all except for Joshua and Caleb (Exodus 1; Numbers 14:29).

When Moses died, Joshua was granted leadership of Israel, and the monumental task of bringing the entire nation into their long-awaited promised inheritance. They would be charged with taking control of the entire land through a series of conquests to drive out the idol-worshipping inhabitants. Since God had destined them to cross over into Canaan from the eastern side of the Jordan River, the first city they would have to conquer was

Jericho. Joshua selected two spies to go over ahead of the rest of the nation and to bring him word about the land and people (Deuteronomy 31:23, Joshua 2:1).

The two men did as they were ordered, and when they came to Jericho, they entered the "house of a harlot named Rahab, and lodged there." Immediately, the king of Jericho received word that the men were at the prostitute's house, and in an act of faith and bravery, she hid them on her roof and lied to the king about their whereabouts (Joshua 2:1-5).

Rahab, hoping to spare her family from the destruction that would soon befall their city, visited the men as they bedded down for the night. She asked them to remember her kindness in hiding them from the king's trackers. She knew that the wrath of God was about to rain down upon her people, and she hoped to be spared.

She testified to the spies about the *terror* that had gripped Jericho and the surrounding cities, for it had been well published about what God had done to the Egyptians forty-years earlier. The people of Jericho also heard the stories about Israel's victories over multiple foreign powers during their desert travels. She shared how the people's "hearts melted" and how the courage of all of the neighboring inhabitants had been downright sapped from them. They had no will or strength to fight. The **terror of the Lord** had done its job, and Jericho ultimately fell to the Israelites (Joshua 2:8-13).

A Refreshed Motivational Secret

While it's true that Jesus stopped Paul on the road to Damascus to save him, it is also true that His first desire was to change Paul's insatiable hatred of the church. Paul had provoked the *terror of the Lord* upon himself, just as the ancient enemies of Israel had. Many may not believe that God still terrorizes the enemies of Israel and His church, but there is nothing in the New Testament to suggest that He doesn't. It may seem as though the divine arm of justice is long and slow, but God always delivers His people from the grasp of evil (2 Thessalonians 1:6; Romans 1:8).

Paul was aware when he penned his words in 2 Corinthians 5 that the terror He had met was present to keep him from continuing his rampage. He also knew that all people would have to take their place before God's judicial bar. He had come to the same conclusion as King Solomon had. Paul was so convinced of this fact that he even compelled fellow Christians to be sober and mindful about every decision and choice they made, because they would be brought under holy scrutinization. Although, all who have trusted in Christ are freely saved, Paul warned that salvation does not mean they are safe and free to do whatever they chose with their lives. He had discovered King Solomon's Secret (2 Corinthians 5:10,11; 1Corinthians 3:13-15).

Paul had allowed *the terror of the Lord* to crush him to death, and a new man was resurrected. God's main objective is, and has always been, to save people, even our worst enemies. This truth is why we must never act with vengeance or repay evil to those who have done evil to us. Paul was consumed with spreading the message of Christ, and he didn't mince words. He was not shy in telling those who rejected the Gospel of what awaited them if they continued shunning the goodness of God found in the death and in the suffering of the Lord. We should be as bold.

If we have a message to preach, and we do, then let it be coupled with an earnest warning that is so passionately expressed that we mark our hearers for eternity. Moreover, our prayers should waft the same passionate savor. Oh, how we should weep for our lost friends and family, knowing that their distance from God means that they are nearer the flames of hell.

If the church-at-large allows (and for the record I believe that it already has) the fear of God to leave its heart and mind, then men and women will be left in a most dangerous, perilous state. I am not suggesting that, if we allow the biblical revelation of the fear of God to be reprised in our hearts, we will be compelled to leave our present lives to become church-planting-evangelists—although it is my prayer that some might. Instead, it is my consuming desire—the yearning that drove me to pen this chapter and this book—that we would find a revived compulsion that mirrors Paul's.

The days of neglecting our neighbor's eternal state should be abandoned, and when *the terror of the Lord* is revived and renewed in us, it shall be. We must, once again, feverishly "pursued men," women and children to know Christ as Paul did. May God convert our chief motivations while He revives our hearts, and may He do it by giving us a fresh revelation of *the Fear of God*.

Chapter Seven
Jesus, on King Solomon's Secret

I had just completed a four week Sunday message series titled *The Fear of God*, and since the feedback was both positive and robust, I was feeling assured that the sermons were a success. I had sensed that God had been guiding me into the study and delivery of the subject for some time, and there was a unique *preaching grace* upon me every week that I had not known for quite a while. In consecutive weeks, some parishioners were moved emotionally and a few wept uncontrollably. In fact, on the last Sunday, while I was giving my final points, one of our members became greatly troubled in her soul and cried out desperately for prayer. This had never happened in the thirteen years prior to that moment. I sensed that it might be a moderate display of personal revival.

However, on the Tuesday following the last sermon, I received a text message from one of my parishioners, a faithful member and a good man, that provoked an immediate angry response within me. I had just given myself to extensive study, prayed earnestly, and poured my heart and soul into delivering each sermon for four straight weeks. I wondered if he had even heard one thing I had said. I felt he was challenging and somewhat correcting me with his question regarding the fear of God.

After I calmed myself and after I considered the person from whom the query came—he is a precious man who would never attempt to hurt me in any way or in any fashion—I realized that God was using him to present me with a golden opportunity to dig further into this wonderful and precious truth. His question was regarding Jesus and His perspective on **worship** versus **the fear of God**. He wondered whether Jesus was more concerned with our worship than He was about us walking in the fear of God. In essence, he was asking if the fear of God was a New Testament subject for which a Christian needed to concern themselves.

It was a valid question and one that needed to be posed. If there is a subject a person feels compelled to preach or write about, he or she might do well to see what the Lord thought about the topic. This is especially true since Jesus, in comparing himself to King Solomon, who we discussed in great detail in chapter one, declared Himself wiser than him. Additionally, Jesus never wavered in His love and respect for the Father, unlike King Solomon (Matthew 12:42).

If King Solomon knew anything about the fear of God, it came from God. Solomon could be no match for the wisdom and knowledge that Jesus possessed on this and on every other subject that has been or will ever be, because Jesus is Emmanuel, God with us. Everything Solomon knew the everlasting Son of God had given him.

I was just heading out of my house on my way to my office at the church when I received the text from the curious parishioner. As I drove, I pondered his question intently. Scriptures began to flood my mind, and by God's grace, I was blessed with illuminating insight. I was anxious to meet with the parishioner in person to share the answer for which he was seeking. Since my thoughts were too lengthy to include in a text message, I decided to write them out upon my classroom sized whiteboard, and I filled every inch of it. We had planned to meet later in the day, and I purposed to be prepared with a thorough reply.

I have given myself, for over half of my life, to the robust and consistent study of the Bible. In the first year after my salvation and conversion I read through the Bible, cover to cover, over five times, and I did not read any other material. On the admonition of my mother, who warned me about the coming of deceivers in latter days, I consumed the Scriptures. She said that I ought to read the Bible through, and when I had finished it, I should read it again, and again, and again. I listened. It may have been the first piece of advice that I heeded from either of my parents from about the age of twelve, and it has served me well. I have read through the Bible at least once per year since then, but most years, I read it twice, and sometimes as much as three times through. I would conservatively guess that I have read the entire Bible over fifty times.

In addition to my daily devotional reading, I also give time to the study of individual books and subjects from the Bible. For example, one year, while studying the love of God, I read the first epistle of John thirty times in thirty days. At another time, I read the Gospels, Matthew through John, three times in thirty days. Also, I have read the New Testament three times in ninety days (about nine chapters per day), all while maintaining my regular reading schedule. I simply cannot get enough of the Scriptures.

I am not sharing this to make myself some kind of Bible elitist that stands above everyone else and for whom there is no questioning or correcting. Not at all. I do not even consider myself a scholar or a theologian, largely because I do not have any formal education. My intentions for opening up my personal study life is to point out that I believe that every word that I speak in reference to the Bible must be accurate and sound. I do not want to be deceived, and I do not want to deceive others. I am still growing and have very much to learn, but whenever I am questioned about a subject that I have given myself to thorough study over, I am passionate about defending it. If we cannot offer a defense of the truths we hold dear, we are apt to eventually waver in our beliefs. However, when I am wrong, I will with equal vigor admit my mistake and seek the correct understanding. God knows I have been wrong more than I care to admit.

Before I answer the question as to whether or not Jesus was more interested in our worship than the fear of God, I have included, with permission, the full message that I received from my parishioner. Bear in mind, I am not trying to prove him wrong, because that would be an impure motive for including this chapter. Rather, what came from His question further mines the depths of truth as it pertains to the fear of God, and I felt it was utterly essential that I include it in this volume. Jesus' thoughts are too important to the subject at hand to overlook, and we could not have an honest look at the fear of God without the Lord's insight. With this in mind, here is the text message:

> "Question: Deuteronomy 6:13 was quoted by Jesus confronting Satan in Matthew 4:10. Why do you think Jesus left out fearing God but emphasized worshipping Him? It seems like Jesus was more interested in the worshipping of our God than the fearing of Him."

Matthew 4 opens with Jesus being driven by the Holy Spirit into the wilderness for a divine showdown with Satan. After fasting from all food for forty straight days, Jesus encountered a series of major temptations at the hands of Satan. In the first temptation, Jesus is asked to turn a rock into bread to immediately satisfy His obvious hunger. Satan, in the second temptation, asks Jesus to throw Himself off of a high point of the Jewish temple in Jerusalem to prove if God would protect Him, and in the last temptation, Jesus is asked to make a pact with Satan: if Jesus would bow in worship to him, Satan would give Jesus immeasurable riches.

In each temptation Jesus prevailed over the enemy by directly quoting the Bible. In a sense, He takes the "sword of the Spirit, which is the Word of God" and thrusts it into Satan to drive Him back, halt his attack, and stymie his advance (Ephesians 6:17).

Satan, being aware of his defeat after the third and final temptation, left Jesus to be cared for and to be strengthened by angelic medics. It was the third temptation that the member of my church had centered his question on:

> "Again, the devil took Him up on an exceedingly high mountain, and showed Him all the kingdoms of the world and their glory. And he said to Him, 'All these things I will give You if You will fall down and worship me.' Then Jesus said to him, 'Away with you, Satan! For it is written, 'You shall worship the Lord your God, and Him only you shall serve.'" – Matthew 4:8-10, NKJV

As stated above, in each of the three temptations, Jesus quoted directly from the Bible, namely the Law of Moses and more specifically the book of Deuteronomy. After the first two temptations, Satan realized that He was not going to get Jesus to waver on His identity and cave in to his evil desires. Rather than try a third round of attempting to get Jesus to doubt His divinity, he decided to sell Jesus on a diabolical partnership for world domination. The only requirement was for Jesus to "fall down and worship" him.

The question that I was posed, "Why do you think Jesus left out fearing God but emphasized worshipping Him," and the ensuing observation, "It seems like Jesus was more interested in the worshipping of our God than the fearing of Him," were both centered on Jesus' reply to Satan's request for worship in which He declared: "Away with you, Satan! For it is written, 'You shall **worship** the Lord your God, and Him only you shall serve.'"

Jesus' biblical rebuke of Satan came from, not one, but two places in the book of Deuteronomy:

> "You shall **fear** the Lord your God and serve Him, and shall take oaths in His name." - Deuteronomy 6:13
>
> "You shall **fear** the Lord your God; you shall serve Him, and to Him you shall hold fast, and take oaths in His name." - Deuteronomy 10:20

A careful reading of the two passages reveals the reason why I was asked about the possibility of Jesus' emphasizing *worship* over the *fear of God*, because it is obvious that Jesus' quotation in Mathew 4:10 uses the word *"worship"* rather than *"fear."*

Before we uncover the reason behind the change from *fear* to *worship,* we must observe that the Holy Spirit authored the Bible and has governed over its various translations through the centuries. We make grievous and grave errors when we offer our private or personal interpretations of biblical texts (2 Peter 1:20).

I am often astounded when I hear people remark that the Bible might say one thing to one person and something different to someone else. In fairness, I know they mean that the Word of God is able to speak to someone at their point of deepest need, but we must be careful not to treat the Holy Scriptures like a magical charm used for mere personal motivation and inspiration. The Bible and its passages, all 31,102 verses, says precisely what it meant to say when the Precious Holy Spirit breathed on forty-plus holy men to author it's sixty-six books. What we *think* it says is of little consequence beyond delightful conversation or friendly debate, and what it *means* to say should always be our final aim and our main objective while studying it.

A Word from a Pastor on Worship

I believe the proliferation of ministries through the use of multimedia is an essential and integral part of advancing the Kingdom of God. However, there is also a danger. When a new and emerging voice finds popular appeal across the Body of Christ, church members of local assemblies are apt to assume that their pastors should be teaching on the same subjects as they do. If, for example, a message on God's love has been dominating Christian airwaves, then it is thought that one's pastor would be wise to immediately fall in line, and when he or she doesn't or does not see the subject in the same light, they aren't held in the same esteem as are the media personalities.

A pastor possesses the role of a shepherd, and it is imperative that each shepherd mind his flock, large or small, and make sure that they are properly nourished. Because of this, parishioners of local assemblies would be wise, while enjoying other outside ministry voices, to regard the words of their shepherds above all others. We learn from the second and third chapters of Revelation that Jesus, who is the Master Shepherd, has a distinct message to seven different localities and the congregations situated in them. It is the same with all modern local assemblies, in that the Lord has a very specific message for each and every one of them, and He speaks specifically to the eldership of each congregation and, more precisely, to its teaching elders. The pastoral team seeks the heart of the Lord for their flock, and it is fair for me to suggest that not one media ministry is overly concerned with the natural and spiritual needs of most local assemblies.

The Lord will not ask any member for permission before disseminating His heart and message for a local church, and He does not need to clear His messages with a single person outside of a governmental leadership role. If a message your pastor is teaching does not fit your latest fancy, I would encourage you to humble yourself and receive it anyway. Tell yourself you will regard your pastor's words as if the Lord Jesus Christ Himself were standing in the pulpit each week delivering the message, and if you cannot do this, I would suggest that you are not in right relationship with your church and, consequently, the Lord. If, every time your shepherd opens his mouth to teach, you are critiquing and judging every word and nuance of the message, then I would suggest you are the problem and not him.

The reason I am belaboring this point is because I am going to make some observations about worship in regard to the fear of God to answer my parishioners question and address his observation. In doing so, I may suggest some things that go crosswise with the prevailing philosophy of your present church context regarding worship and the fear of God, and I do not want what I am writing to be held in higher esteem than what your pastor has taught or is teaching on the subject. In fact, I would recommend providing a copy of this work for your leadership at your church if you feel it may bless them, but please do not allow anything in this book or in this chapter to create an inner friction if it does not necessarily correspond to the house of worship you are connected to.

This is not to suggest that erroneous teaching should not be challenged. Not at all, but you should always do so prayerfully, in a humble manner, and through the proper channels, as my friend did in sending me his text.

To begin, *worship* is not exclusively singing nor is it a point that is reached in a public gathering of Christians. The primary, prevailing view of worship for many believers is that it has to do with singing. Additionally, most churches call the song service portion of their corporate expression the *worship service*. There is a trend among many local assemblies to have a *Night of Worship*, which means there will only be singing without preaching. Also, there is a distinction between faster music, which is typically called *praise*, and slower music, which gets the *worship* designation. Because of this misuse of the phrase, most of us have come to believe that to worship means to sing to God. The terms are viewed synonymously.

While some churches call the song portion of their gatherings the *worship service*, others yet, title the entire service as an expression of worship: Singing, the collection of offerings, giving and receiving the sacraments (communion time), the message and the final appeal for receiving Jesus. A common invitation adorning many church signs that hold this view is: "Come worship with us." There is an essential problem with this second perspective on worship as well. Specifically, a person is left with the impression that the only place one can worship is in a building designed exclusively for that purpose.

One view says, "Singing is worship," and the other view says, "Worship must be done here with us." Neither of the two views are necessarily wrong, but neither is entirely accurate.

An entire volume can and should be dedicated to the subject of worship. In fact, there are many wonderful works that have already been published on the topic. However, since worship is not the core assignment of this book, I will not be able to give time to a total biblical discovery of the term and its scriptural usage. With that said, there is a Bible passage (actually the passage is repeated in three different places, but we will examine only one of them) that begins the process of unearthing what it means to worship and why Jesus may have chosen to use the word in place of fear.

> "O worship the Lord in the beauty of holiness: fear before him, all the earth." - Psalm 96:9, KJV

While it is true there are plenty of verses that deal with the specific act or expression of worship, and to be sure, it is both an action and an expression, notice this verse says nothing about where to worship, but simply how to worship, and singing is excluded. We are instructed to "worship the Lord in the beauty of holiness," with the secondary admonition to "fear before him." With this verse from Psalms, we begin to uncover a possible reason as to why Jesus changed the word *fear* to *worship*.

Three Assumptions Debunked

We expose the ***first*** of ***three assumptions*** that my parishioner held, along with most Bible reference materials, and that is: **Jesus was exclusively quoting from Deuteronomy 6:13**.

If you search most commentaries and read from the majority of Scriptural reference books, you will find that there is unanimous agreement that Jesus was citing Deuteronomy 6:13, but only a few point out that He was also quoting from 10:20 of the same book. It is not my intention to bog my readers down with sundry details and a minutia of points and facts. However, it is essential to understand that it was not uncommon for Jesus to quote verses from multiple places in the Old Testament and to do it in a way in which He condenses several verses into one quotation. For example, when Jesus proclaimed Himself as Messiah for the first time in Luke 4:18 and 19, He does so by taking three different verse locations: two from Isaiah 49:8-9 and 61:1-2 and a third from Daniel 9:24.

Therefore, it is not unacceptable, without being dogmatic, to suggest that Jesus, at the very least, had Psalm 96:9 in mind when He was rebuking the devil.

While chapter and verse numberings make Bible reading more manageable and citations more specific, they were not introduced into printed editions of the Bible until the fifteenth century. Today, most of us would never quote the Bible without giving chapter and verse. As well, the most astute preachers are ever faithful to give reference numbers during their Bible lessons. This was not the case with the believers of the early Bible era, and it was not the case with Jesus. In His famous sermon on the mount—Matthew 5, 6 and 7—He quotes the Old Testament several times without giving reference numbers.

While I would not be willing to state in emphatic terms that Jesus was quoting Psalm 96:9 in addition to Deuteronomy 6:13 and 10:20, I do not believe that anyone could prove that He was not. The reason for this rests in what it means to "worship the Lord in the beauty of holiness." Notice that it does not say to "worship the Lord *for* His beautiful holiness," but to worship Him "*in* the beauty of holiness." This means that it is beautiful in the sight of God when His people live out their lives before Him in a holy manner, and God calls it worship when His people live holy. Why do people choose to live holy instead of godless and unholy? Because of their reverence and respect for God and their deep regard for Him. They do it because they love and fear God.

To be holy means to be separated from one thing unto something else. For example, marriage is called *holy matrimony* because two people have decided, as an act of their free will, to be separated from all other potential lovers and suiters and to be exclusively separated for only one person for life. It is the same with our God. He calls us holy because He has separated us by and through the blood of His Son, Jesus, but we also must decide to live separated lives unto God as holy children. Yes, before God, we are holy and blameless, but He expects that reality to be lived out daily (Ephesians 1:4).

Consider the following:

> "Because we have these promises, dear friends, let us cleanse ourselves from everything that can defile our body or spirit. And let us work toward complete holiness because **we fear God.**" – 2 Corinthians, NLT

God finds our lives beautiful when we have been washed in the blood of His Son and regenerated by His Holy Spirit. He is greatly pleased and honored when we walk out and work out that reality, daily, by ridding ourselves of every defilement.

God calls it worship when someone bows their knee and confesses that Jesus is Lord, and He receives worship when His child chooses to reject this world and all of its perversions. If a sinner, who has continued to reject the sacrifice of Christ, were to sing the latest and hottest so-called worship song, it would not make his singing worship any more than sitting in a burger joint would make him a hamburger. A worship song is only worship when it is sung through lips that have confessed Jesus as Lord and have renounced the continued practice of sinful pleasures.

Worshiping "the Lord in the beauty of holiness" means that God sees the totality of our lives as an act and expression of worship unto Him. When we sleep and when we arise, it is worship. When we go to a job in a factory or in an office tower and give an honest day's labor, it is worship. When we honor our nuptials while others count theirs with little regard, it is worship. When we show up at our child's ballgame, recital, play ball, or play in the recital, it is worship. It is no less worship for a blood-washed, God-honoring family to be on vacation together than it is for them to be in a church service together. The sum total of our lives lived out in the fear of God is called worship, and it is likely that Jesus had this thought on His mind when He rebuked the devil.

The *second assumption* embedded in the text message I received is that **Jesus is more interested in worship than in the fear of God**. First, it is no more fair to assume this than it would be to assume the opposite, specifically that Jesus is more interested in the fear of God than He is worshipping God. A very simple rule for building opinions or for formulating doctrines is to allow the Bible to interpret the Bible. My parishioner, as well meaning as he was, had not gone far enough in the Gospels before settling on his observation.

There is a mad rush in some Christian circles to view everything from the Old Testament as outmoded and antiquated. They see God in the Old Testament as angry, irritated and grumpy, while seeing Him in the New Testament as kind, patient, caring and loving. It is almost as if they are saying, through this false image of God, that He is manic in His temperament. One of the characteristics of God's eternal unblemished nature is that He is immutable, which means He does not change. If He was capable of changing, then we would have no assurances at all from Him or His Word. He simply could not be trusted.

We have all encountered the pain that came from people who made promises to us, but broke their word for a variety of reasons. How then could we be expected to trust God if we cannot know that He means to fulfill His promises to us? If He is just like the people that didn't stick with the commitments they made to us, how could we be sure, for example, that the Cross is all sufficient? We cannot, for we would have justifiable cause to interrogate and question its efficaciousness.

God has not changed, and the Cross is the place where the full demonstration of God's wrath, coupled with His limitless love, was put on full display. The totality of His vengeance was poured upon our Lord, and we have yet to fully comprehend what that idea even means, much less firmly grasp its implications. I am frightened by the thought of what it will be like on the Day of Judgement for those who have heard the Gospel of Jesus Christ presented with clarity and yet remain unmoved by it. This rejection will be to the catastrophic peril of untold millions and perhaps billions of eternally damned souls. The Christian is in possession of the single most important eternal information the world has ever known: That a person can escape when they die the eternal torments of hell by trusting Christ Jesus as Lord and Savior.

What then is the *fear of God* if it isn't a clear and perfect understanding of eternal damnation?

Charles Spurgeon, the eighteenth century pastor from England who was known as the *Prince of Preachers,* once said, "If sinners be damned, at least let them leap to Hell over our dead bodies. And if they perish, let them perish with our arms wrapped about their knees, imploring them to stay. If hell must be filled, let it be filled in the teeth of our exertions, and let not one go unwarned and unprayed for."

In my estimation, and it is only my humble observation, much of what is preached in pulpits at the present time gives little mention of hell and the *fear of God* and does even less to move people beyond emotional decisions for Jesus into true conversions. I've come to this conclusion by perusing the various Christian networks that adorn satellite and cable television, along with sitting in several conferences with many recognizable and internationally known ministers of the Gospel.

The net result of largely ignoring these very important realities is that many believers have gotten lax in their life choices, soft in their prayers, and half-dead in their evangelizing. There is something profoundly motivating in the revelation that Jesus suffered, died and rose again to rescue us from the flames of hell, which provokes incredible expressions of devotion and love, fires up the prayer life, and fuels our soul winning efforts. We must not lose sight of these great and precious truths.

Jesus spoke about the subject of hell and eternal separation from God in twelve different verses (60 in total if one takes His indirect comments in to account, which is roughly 3% of everything recorded that He said). In comparison He spoke about worship in a total of eight verses that specifically used the word *worship*. I don't believe it would be fair to suggest that Jesus cared about one over the other simply from a disparity in the amount of times He mentions them. For example, I believe a biblical understanding of marriage was and is important to Jesus, yet He spoke even less about it than He did *hell* and *worship*. Nevertheless, we cannot conclude that it was less or more important to Him simply based on the volume in which He spoke about it. We can only extract what He thought about a topic by what He actually said about it, while also considering the topic from Genesis to Revelation.

In Luke 24, Jesus, post-resurrection, encounters two men journeying to a village called Emmaus, and they did not recognize Him. Since they were downcast due to His suffering, death, and rumors that Jesus was alive, Jesus asked about their present sadness. They were shocked, because they thought everyone who was anyone would know what had taken place recently in Jerusalem. At that moment, Jesus, still unrecognizable to them, opened up the Scriptures concerning His life and sufferings. In fact, verse 27 says, "He expounded to them in all the Scriptures the things concerning Himself." Notice that Jesus took the time to look at the topic of His life from the whole of Scripture, and it is critical that we follow His example in exploring a subject from more than one place in the Word of God.

This leads us, invariably, to the ***third assumption*** that was in the question and observation that I received via text message: **Jesus *deliberately changed a verse* to suit a different theological position than the one clearly expressed throughout Scripture.**

I have already shown that Jesus' example proves otherwise, yet we should also consider that He said of Himself that He did not come to earth to "destroy the Law or the Prophets…but to fulfill" and that there would not be the slightest detail that would pass from the law until it was thoroughly, totally and completely fulfilled by Him. He would not change what he had come to fulfill, and let us never forget that He is the embodiment of the Word of God, and to change a Scripture would be to change Himself, which He could not do (Matthew 5:17,18; John 1:1-14).

To assume that "Jesus is more interested in worship than in the fear of God" from one encounter that He had with Satan does not even hold up against the most liberal, lax, or slapdash Bible study standards. Those who consider themselves biblical novices would do well to spend just a few more minutes exploring *thoughts* or *feelings* about a scriptural text before claiming possible special knowledge.

Jesus, Worship and the Fear of God

Probably the most damaging piece of evidence against the observation I received from my friend is that Jesus actually mentions *hell* and the *fear of God* in the same verse and at least confirms that the *fear of God* is as equally important to Him as *worship*. Here is the verse:

> "Dear friends, don't be afraid of those who want to kill your body; they cannot do any more to you after that. But I'll tell you whom to fear. Fear God, who has the power to kill you and then throw you into hell. Yes, he's the one to fear." – Luke 12:4-5, NLT

From these two verses, we surmise that the *fear of God* was a subject that Jesus considered important enough to bring up in conjunction with the topic of *hell*. For Jesus, the Creator of all things seen and unseen, hell was no place that any man should ever want to be. Hell was exclusively created for the devil and the angels that followed him in his failed heavenly coup. Mankind, having submitted to Satan's rule over them in their Edenic treason, chose another eternal destination in place of the paradise of God. Jesus understands well the inescapable horrors of hell and does not desire a single soul to suffer there (Matthew 25:41).

God is the giver of life, and He has power over all flesh. He can give a single command and a man would cease, that very instant, to exist on this planet. Additionally, God is the only One that can give the edict for a soul to be damned, and He is the only One that can provide the way of escape.

Luke 12:4 and 5 is Jesus' way of telling us to respect God and reverence Him as the Author and Giver of all life and to give Him deference, seeing that He can command, and a soul will be damned forever. Even if someone were to kill you for spreading the Gospel, don't fear that or them. Live fearless, because your entrance into heaven is assured, but if you allow yourself to fear men, you cannot fear God properly and do what He asks of you.

So why did Jesus replace the word **fear** with **worship** when quoting Deuteronomy 6:13 and 10:20 while rebuking Satan in Matthew 4:10?

The Greek word translated as *worship* in Mathew 4:10, *pros-kü-né-ō,* meant to the people of the East to fall upon the knees and touch the ground with the forehead as an act of profound reverence in showing homage to a person of superior rank. Recall that it was to Satan's request for Jesus to "fall down and worship" him that Jesus replied with the rebuke, "Away with you, Satan! For it is written, 'You shall worship the Lord your God, and Him only you shall serve.'"

By asking Jesus to "**fall down** and worship" him, Satan was, in effect, asking Jesus to acknowledge Him as God—pure and simple. He wasn't requesting for Jesus to sing Him a so-called "worship" song. No, He wanted Jesus to pay Him the deference and reverence due and reserved only for the Living God, and that is why Jesus' response takes on profound importance. When Satan asked for worship from the Son of God, it was in continuance of his ongoing rebellion against heaven and with the hopes that Jesus would satisfy Satan's insatiable, yet impossible, desire to dethrone God (Isaiah 14).

He wanted Jesus to bow His knee, touch the ground with His head, and affirm Satan's godhood over humanity. Had he succeeded in getting Jesus to take the bait, he would have conquered God in the process. It was a tremendous gamble that the Father had permitted in allowing His Son to be tempted in this manner, but it would not be for naught. Jesus succeeded where the first Adam had failed.

Jesus changed the words around because to *fear God* is the highest expression of *worship* that we can give God. In other words, we *worship* God when we *fear God*.

English Baptist pastor, Bible scholar, and theologian, John Gill, in referring to Jesus' choice to change *fear* to *worship*, once said, "To fear the Lord, and to worship Him, is the same thing."

What Electricity Taught Me about the Fear of God

I worked as an electrical apprentice for two years for the world's largest steel manufacturing company. My journeymen masters taught me to fear electricity. I do not mean that they taught me to cower and cringe away in torment. Rather, they instructed me to have a healthy respect for it. They told me horrible stories of men who had gotten too comfortable with the power they were working with and they paid with their health and some with their lives. Since I did not want to die in that mill and desired to make it home to my young family, I listened and obeyed.

At times, we worked with voltage that would kill an elephant in a millisecond. Their warnings to me and my fellow apprentices were no laughing matter. We had *lock-out* protocols and procedures we had to employ before we could work on certain machines. At times we had to pull fuses before we could replace wires. All of this was done to keep us safe and to keep us alive.

I learned three very important lessons about why it is important to *fear* the power of electricity and consequently any power, including God's power:

- Fear helps us respect protective boundaries necessary to keep us safe
- Fear brings us into a right, proper and healthy relationship with the power resource
- Fear helps us derive the max benefit from the power resource

In the department that I worked in at the steel mill, we often had to visit the power supply room which was roughly the size of a football field. The floors were immaculate, being swept and mopped during every shift by a team of men dedicated to keeping mill dust and metal shavings off the floor, which could be a problematic electrical conductor. Within the power room were three humongous generators, a couple that supplied electricity and one that was reserved for backup. The generators supplied so much electricity that, under the laws of our state, power companies were expected to purchase the excess electricity that they produced.

There were a few times during my tenure when we had to do work in the power room for various reasons. We were expected to pull a 13,000 volt power switch that was the size of a small refrigerator. Around the switch there was a warning barrier that no one was permitted to cross without wearing the proper equipment. Even beyond the barrier, the hair on our arms would stand up, and an odd tingling sensation would tickle our heads. The power of the voltage was evident to us all.

Before we could pull the switch, we had to be static free so that the electricity didn't *jump* the switch and kill us instantly. Then, we had to wear very thick rubber gloves that came up to our shoulders, a rubberized apron, and a special helmet with a clear shield. We had to be standing upon a rubberized mat—every item was free of any conductive material. Then, with non-conducting tongs, we were able to pull the switch, which would cut the power to the area where we needed to work. In the final step, we had to check if the supply of power was dead with very long voltage meter sticks that resembled a child's fourth of July toy or gadget. When we were done with the job, we repeated everything in reverse.

The boundaries that we were expected to respect were not in place because someone was grouchy and did not want us to enjoy the electrical power. Instead, the boundaries were there for our safety. God is Holy and His power exceeds any power on earth. This point must not be missed. No one can see God in His unveiled splendor and survive it. No one can meet His holiness with the static of sin and not have His power *jump* upon them to their detriment. **Fear helps us respect protective boundaries necessary to keep us safe.**

Had we not shown respect and regard for the commands of the men in charge of keeping us safe from the indiscriminate power of 13,000 volts of electricity, we could not have remained healthy. By honoring their words, trusting their guidance, and heeding the sad tales of the men that went before us – for whom becoming overly lax in their behavior resulted in their peril – we were able to make it home to our families every evening.

We needed that electricity to sustain the mill just as we need God to sustain our lives. We cannot live without Him just as we could not produce steel for our customers without the electricity. When that mill ran, we were able to provide an above average lifestyle for our families. A right relationship with the power source that drove the mill was needed so that we could continue our blessed livelihood. We will never receive all that God has intended for us if we are outside of His divine order. We will not respect His order if we do not respect Him. **Fear brings us into a right, proper and healthy relationship with the power source.**

As stated, the mill was inextricably bound to the health of its supply of power. We were the keepers, the guardians if you will, of that power supply. Those steel workers, without saying it, knew that the comfort of their families was dependent upon us keeping that mill up and running. We knew that we were needed and we relished the fact. As necessary as we were, we understood that we were no good without that electricity. That power made everything in that mill work, and we had to maintain its flow. If we didn't or couldn't, we stayed long after the line workers left, ensuring that the power would be back to good working order for the next shift. That electricity was worth its weight in gold, and when it was working well, we were all paid well. **Fear helps us derive the max benefit from the power source.**

At the risk of sounding superficial, I must stress the importance of maintaining a healthy respect for God, which, in turn, results in the maximization of His many benefits. There is no "good thing" that He withholds from "him that walks uprightly" (Psalm 84:11).

There is no getting around our responsibility to be obedient. It is obedience that brings blessings. To be sure, our righteous status and position before God is tied only to our faith in Christ's redemptive work on the Cross. However, if we do not walk in the light of His Word, we will not see our prayers answered and the blessings flow (John15:7).

Some families have known a stubborn or rebellious child who had to be cut off from parental good graces so that they might come to a place of humility and responsibility. Their last name may have been the same as their father, but they could not enjoy the father's blessing because of an unruly lifestyle. We must continue to walk in the *fear of God* if we are going to maintain the max benefit of our relationship with Him.

Honoring God pleases Him. If we claim to love Him and very often boldly confess that He loves us—and He most assuredly does—then why wouldn't we continue to do all that is within our will and ability to rightly pay Him in reverential life-worship?

Let us move beyond mere lip-service and properly worship God by making sure that we appropriately respect Him in all manner of living. May we be circumspect in our personal choices and our treatment of others as a way to express His fear continually. May the Holy Spirit keep us from the deception that we are permitted to excuse our continual practice of shameful behaviors, simply because we believe the Lord to be inexhaustibly gracious. God forbid.

We cannot claim to worship God when we refuse to fear and tremble before Him. We should not claim to worship Him with the same lips that love a steady diet of frequently cursing our neighbors. Holiness is the divine barometer that reflects one's atmospheric health in regard to one's respect for God. To fear God is the highest expression of worship we can give Him.

To Jesus, to fear God is to worship Him.

Chapter Eight
The Secret Ingredient to Successful Prayer

If there has been a failure in the life of a Christ follower, be it a relational, a financial, or a career failure, it is highly probable that the breakdown began where there was an absence or lack of prayer. We have previously learned that asking God for wisdom is essential to successful prayer. Even if we are simply praying for God's wisdom in a situation, we are still praying. Prayer is essential, and not praying is dangerous.

I once had the honor of spending a little time with a bishop from Uganda whose ministry began at the age of seventeen when he raised a young girl from the dead. I was in my early thirties at the time, and he was several years older. His skin was of a shiny, even and deep blackish-brown hue. He wore a tightly cropped thin mustache and chin hair. The character of his chiseled cheek bones and almond shaped, deeply-set eyes spoke of much travel and little sleep. He was tall and handsomely dressed in traditional East African garb which lent him a stately, almost, royal demeanor. It was also evident that his shoes were not purchased at a discount outlet. I was deeply impressed by him. He was excellent in presentation, and the presence of God emanated from him.

As he was preparing to preach a live segment for an international Christian television network, I was anxious to ask him something—anything. I noticed he did not speak to the hosting pastors unless he was spoken to, so I knew I had to pick the right question at the right moment. I felt nervous. I wanted to wait until we were alone in the green-room. Directors, producers and other members of the network's team came in and out constantly, and I was worried that I'd never get the chance.

His reputation had preceded him, and I knew he was a much sought after speaker, published author, and had one of, if not *the,* largest congregations on the African continent. At that time, he had planted over 500 other churches across his continent.

I watched him as he perused the notes that he would soon be using to deliver his address. He focused on his yellow legal pad with an unflinching intensity, and he barely moved while he sat alone on an over-sized leather couch, his right leg draped over his left. From outside the room, I heard the program begin, and the flow of visitors stanched, and I knew that I had better take my chance then or lose my opportunity forever. I had settled upon the one question I believed was the most pertinent to my life and ministry. I said, "Bishop, may I ask you a question, sir?"

"Of course, you may," the bishop said. He spoke with a gravelly and whisper-like tone, and his voice was beautifully seasoned from over-use. His accent was thick, but understandable.

"What part has prayer played in the success of your life and ministry?" I said with a child-like inquisitiveness.

"Oh," said the Bishop, "prayer is everything. When we breathe, we pray, and when we pray, we breathe." He stood up and walked over to where his attaché case was positioned. "Come, let me show you something." I got up and hurried over to look at a brochure he had pulled from his case. He said, "You see this?" As he tapped the images of the interior and exterior of a massive auditorium. I could tell it was designed for a church, yet it had the appearance of a slightly smaller sporting arena.

I said, "Yes sir."

"We build with prayer. Cash. No American dollars. My country is not rich like yours. One man I never met in the Philippines wake up in the middle of the night, and God tell him to send me one million dollars. We owe no money on the building. We do it all with prayer."

The bishop and I exchanged a few more words, and while we were concluding our discussion, the hosting pastor walked in, and I could tell that I had agitated him for bothering the bishop while he was preparing to speak. I felt bad, but didn't let his angst bother me, because I needed to hear the words, "Prayer is everything."

The host left the room and had an assistant come escort me to my special seating assignment. I later apologized to him. I have never spoken to the bishop since that time, but it wasn't necessary, because I believe that it was a divine appointment, and over the years, I have come to learn how rare such visits are.

Jesus, the Son of God, depended greatly on a consistent and continual life of prayer. In the Gospel writings (Matthew, Mark, Luke and John), we find Jesus praying late into the evening, very early in the morning, and leaning upon heaven during His most excruciating moments. In fact, after witnessing the powerful teachings and demonstrations of His evangelistic campaigns and the miracles He performed on a regular basis, the twelve disciples asked Him to teach them to pray. I marvel that He hadn't made it a point to teach them how to pray until they asked. It is probable He waited for them to ask, knowing people learn best when their interest in a subject is at a heightened state (Matthew 14:23, Mark 1:35, Luke 22:41 & 11:1).

Besides limited or scant use, many people find their lives deficient of prayer successes through a lack of knowledge or proper instruction. Prayer as defined in the Bible, in a general sense, is simply the communication that mankind has with their Creator. Prayer is spiritual communication.

However, there is a problem when we inadvertently apply the specifics of certain *types* of prayer to every other kind. For example, the various and unique aspects of the *prayer of faith* should not be used in the *intercessory prayer* category. (Because different Bible teachers use various terms that mean the same thing, please do not get hung up on the prayer category designations I have chosen to use for this chapter.)

The prayer of faith need not be prayed more than once, because it rests on the clearly revealed promises of Scripture. However, the prayer of intercession is different. It requires continual persistence until the victory has been had. Also, the prayer of faith is usually prayed for one's self—with certain exceptions—while intercessory prayer is, more often than not, prayed for others. When a person mistakenly asks for something repeatedly that has been clearly guaranteed, it may be a sign of doubt. With God's promises, we simply need to receive what has been given and remain in a state of gratitude until it manifests. In contrast, with intercession, continual asking is absolutely necessary.

Here is how the prayer of faith looks in comparison to intercession:

- **THE PRAYER OF FAITH**: "Father, I thank You that You promised to meet my every need through the abundant riches of Your Son Jesus (Philippians 4:19). Therefore, I ask You to increase my monthly income by $100.00. In Jesus' name I pray!"

- **HOW YOU WOULD PRAY THE NEXT DAY**: "Father, I thank You that You have heard me concerning the increase to my monthly income, and I praise You. Since You always hear me and Your Word has promised me that You would meet my need, I receive that it's mine in Jesus' Name, Amen!" (You are not re-asking; you are thanking until it comes.)

- **INTERCESSION**: "Father, I ask You to guide my president and congressional leaders with wisdom, knowledge and understanding by Your Holy Spirit. Please protect them and deliver them from those that would seek to harm them or their families. Forgive them, Lord, when they are not obedient to Your will and reject Your Word, knowingly or unknowingly. May our nation remember where all its blessings have flowed from and return to You in humility. I pray in Jesus' Name.

- **HOW YOU WOULD PRAY THE NEXT DAY**: Repeat the above.

You'll notice that both types of prayers have in common a direct address to God the Father, and both conclude with *"in the name of Jesus."* Every kind of prayer will share these essential qualities. The difference, however, is that *the prayer of faith* rested on Philippians 4:19 as the guarantee of its answer and, therefore, did not need to be asked again, but the *intercessor's prayer* is repeated as often as is necessary. There are no specific promises that guarantee that leaders of nations will be godly or righteous, that they'll be protected, or that they will lead with heavenly wisdom, and it is our job to pray with constancy that they will.

I have been asked, on more than one occasion, if it is wrong to repeatedly ask God for the same thing. I usually reply that it depends on what it is that is being asked. I love to remind people that their Heavenly Father loves them intensely and is never bothered when they ask Him multiple times for anything. He will not condemn His children any more than a loving and caring parent would an indefatigable child. My children have often worn me down with their appeals to satisfy their desires. However, if He has already showed us in the Scriptures what His will is concerning our request, then we would do well to simply believe Him. Faith pleases Him (Mark 11:24; Hebrews 11:6; 1 John 5:14-15).

While there are at least seven different types or categories of prayer in the Bible (the prayer of faith/petition, of consecration/dedication, of confession, of declaration, of repentance, of praise, and of intercessory/importunate prayer), space would elude us in this chapter to cover the full subject. There are wonderful books available today that cover prayer in depth. Instead, we will zero our efforts on the particulars associated with intercession, and after we have laid a strong foundation for effectiveness, I will, in the next chapter, give seven steps for praying successfully for your loved one. I won't repeat the various reasons why it is paramount that the *fear of God* be operational in our personal lives, because this book has been dedicated to that end, but we cannot overlook the downright necessity that it will play, especially through prayer, in seeing those who are precious to us surrendered to Christ.

Before King Solomon, There Was Abraham

Most are familiar with the notable Bible personality Abraham, who has been called, by many, the *Father of Faith*. Christianity, Judaism and Islam all claim Abraham as the founder and father of their religions. All told, almost four billion people alive today look to Abraham as a primary source in their connection with God.

Abraham, whose name was Abram at the time, was called by God at the age of seventy-five to leave the comfort of his family, friends and home. The city he left was called Ur of the Chaldees, and it was located in the southeastern region of modern day Iraq. Abram obeyed and headed west in the direction of present day Israel. In Ur, he was likely a financially stable and prosperous business man, but God called him to begin a nomadic life of deep trust in Him. Since Abram and his wife Sarai were childless and his nephew Lot was fatherless, they took him along in pursuit of God's destiny in Canaan (Genesis 11:26-32; 12:1-6).

Eventually, Lot and Abram had to part ways due to the abundance of their livestock, quarreling between their herdsmen, and the inability of the land to sustain both of their herds. Lot chose the direction of Sodom and Gomorrah, and Abram went in the opposite direction. Lot chose the region of Sodom and Gomorrah because it was lush and well-watered and left Abram to the desert regions of Canaan (Genesis 13:5-13).

God promised Abram, who after many years was still childless, that He would give him a son to whom he could pass on the blessing of the *Promised Land.* However, more years passed, and with the aging of their bodies, the promise of a son seemed, to both Abram and Sarai, less and less likely. In desperation, Sarai asked Abram to take her personal servant Hagar, an Egyptian woman they had acquired in Egypt, and have a child with her. Abram agreed, married Hagar, and she became pregnant. Hagar was an ancient version of a surrogate mother, and Sarai had every intention of raising the child as her own. However, because Sarai treated Hagar contemptuously, Hagar fled the camp (Genesis 12:7; 16:1-6).

After an angel commanded her to return, Hagar complied and fully submitted herself to her mistress, Sarai. Shortly after, she bore a son whom Abram named Ishmael. Abram, now 86 years old and content to make Ishmael his sole heir, settled on the fact that Sarai would never conceive. Ishmael, Abram decided, along with his decedents would inherit everything, including all the land of Canaan (Genesis 16:7-16; 17:18).

Soon after, God visited Abram to inform him that He was changing his name to reflect his destiny. No longer would he be called Abram, which meant *exalted father*, but his name would forever be Abraham, *the father of a multitude*. Additionally, Sarai (*my princess*), would be called Sarah (*princess of a multitude*), because it was Jehovah's eternal desire to make Sarah the mother from which the promised son would come forth. In addition to His plan to satisfy Abraham's desire for a descendent to inherit his house and the land—the land of Canaan would later become the nation of Israel—God also intended to bring forth the Messiah of the world through the two of them (Genesis 17:1-19).

Jehovah again visited Abraham to confirm His will to give him an heir through Sarah. However, Abraham begged God to make Ishmael the heir to his wealth, land and yet-to-be-fulfilled-promises. God said no. God said that Sarah, in spite of being childless and barren, would conceive and bare Abraham a son. Abraham laughed out loud at the thought that he and Sarah would have a son together, especially after the passing of so many years, and God took note of his chuckle (Genesis 17:16-22).

Thirteen years after the birth of Ishmael, Abraham, in spite of being 99 years old—his body, old and near dead—chose to believe God, and nine months later, at the age of 100, he was given a son with Sarah. God commanded them to name him Isaac, whose name means *laughter*. God had the last laugh.

There is little doubt that Abraham had a robust faith in God. He left his homeland upon hearing God's rather vague command as to where he was to go, trusting God to lead his every step. He was able to sire a son while he and his wife had long passed the years when the desire for sexual intimacy was the highest and their bodies could still produce offspring. The writer of the New Testament book of Hebrews included Abraham and Sarah in the eleventh chapter as magnificent examples of great faith. The Apostle Paul dedicated significant portions of *his* writings to the examination of Abraham's faith and its impact on the manifestation of Christ's life, death and resurrection. The world has been left better because Abraham believed God and found favor with Him (Roman 4; Galatians 3; Hebrews 11:8, 17).

Yet as well known and thoroughly recorded as Abraham's faith in God has been, few have noted that Abraham was a man of powerful intercession to the point where God conceded His plans and yielded to Abraham's humble demands. God was mightily impacted by Abraham's appeals. We can learn much about intercessory prayer from his example. However, before we can unpack his life of prayer, there is one more critical event, indeed the most pivotal, in the life of Abraham which would test his faith on a level he had not previously experienced. Passing this test would leave him nearly alone among an elite class of believers. This event would reveal an essential element about Abraham's character, the character that is greatly needed to be a successful intercessor and person of faith.

The Secret to Passing Great Tests

Many years after Isaac's birth, the Lord came to Abraham and commanded him to sacrifice Isaac as a burnt offering. Isaac was the son of his intense love and desire, the fulfillment of twenty-five long years of holding on to God's vow, even through moderate trepidation and uncertainty (Genesis 22:2).

Isaac was Abraham's dream come true, and his soul was bound up in his son.

The very first time the word *love* is mentioned in the Bible, it is mentioned in conjunction with Abraham's love for Isaac and God's call to sacrifice Abraham's son. God would sacrifice the Son of His *love* two-thousand years later. By applying the Bible study technique known as the *Law of First Mention*, which is used to get at the root of the inherent meaning of a biblical doctrine by finding a word or phrase as it is first used, we are able to clearly define love as **sacrificial**. In fact, the truth that love is first and foremost sacrificial is something that is carried through the entirety of the biblical record, beginning with Abraham and Isaac:

> "Take your son, your only son—yes, Isaac, whom you love so much—and go to the land of Moriah. Go and sacrifice him as a burnt offering on one of the mountains, which I will show you." - Genesis 22:2, NLT

God was setting a precedent that would be carefully recorded for future generations until the time of Christ's coming. His life would be the consummate demonstration of love.

Most confuse love with a feeling or an emotion, but that is the lowest understanding of love that there is in the universe. This misunderstanding has ended many marriages. Love is not, first, romance, though love will have in a romantic relationship romantic interludes. However, there will be seasons within every romantic relationship where the feelings of romance have assuaged. This does not mean that there should cease to be love. In fact, in moments where there has been the absence of *loving feelings*, there should be the expression of self-sacrifice. Love should actually deepen during these times.

A wife, for example, may be tempted to explore other relationships in pursuit of the euphoria associated with the romance she had at the onset of her courtship, but instead, sacrifices her desires in favor of honoring the eternal covenant she made on her wedding day. A spouse who confuses romance for love will always look to their partner to gratify their needs instead of living to gratify their spouse. When two people in a marriage know and practice this truth, there will be heaven in their home.

Genesis 22 makes no mention of Abraham discussing his plans to travel to Moriah with Sarah or telling her of the reason he was heading there. Sarah likely would resist any attempt to bring harm to Isaac, especially since Isaac was her one and only child. Instead, this was an exclusive father and son expedition into the unknown that would test both Abraham and Isaac.

Depending on what commentary is consulted, we can come away with a rough estimate of Isaac's age as being around 33, hardly the age where a son wouldn't question a father's actions or where he couldn't fight his father off if he needed to.

We've already established that Abraham had another son named Ishmael. However, God does not acknowledge him, in Genesis 22:2, as a legitimate claimant of the promises given *to* and made *with* Abraham. As far as God was concerned, he had never given Abraham permission to produce an heir with anyone other than Sarah.

While polygamy was widely practiced in the Bible, it was never sanctioned, endorsed or encouraged as a legitimate marital institution. Sarah was Abraham's wife, and it was through her that the Lord had always intended to fulfill His future plans. God never condemned the two of them for Abraham's marriage to Hagar or get angry over birth of Ishmael, but neither did He condone the haphazard act. He never revamps or revises His covenants when people get antsy and try, in futility, to help Him move His plans along a little faster.

Abraham understood the significance of the Lord's directive and was faced with a very serious dilemma. In the first place, how could Jehovah satisfy His commitments if Isaac was dead, and secondly, if He had planned on resurrecting Isaac after being sacrificed, how could he do it if Isaac's corpse was burned down to an ash heap? These were sobering questions to consider.

Abraham had a grave situation before him, because if God was not going to accept Ishmael, then He would need to do something supernatural with Isaac to make good on His promises. Abraham would need to rest his faith on the Word that God had given him time and again over the years. Abraham had two choices: obey and offer Isaac or disobey and reject God. The first option would require something greater than the faith it took to produce the life of Isaac in the first place. With the second, it would mean a forfeiture of everything He had trusted God to do up until that time and into the future. This was Abraham's greatest test.

Abraham wasted no time weighing his options and obeyed the next morning. Upon rising very early, he "saddled his donkey, and took two of his young men with him, and Isaac his son; and he split the wood for the burnt offering, and arose and went to the place of which God had told him." After a three-day journey, Abraham noticed the region of Moriah—modern day Jerusalem—in the distance.

What Abraham said next was clear proof of the depth of His faith in God to fulfill and satisfy His promise to him:

> And Abraham said to his young men, "Stay here with the donkey; the lad [young man] and I will go yonder and

> worship, and we will come back to you." – Genesis 22:5, NKJV, words in brackets added

Abraham made a powerful declaration that must not be lightly regarded. Consider that he fully intended on giving Isaac as a burnt offering and he verified the fact when he arose early to chop wood for the occasion. He was fully invested. He was committed to driving a knife into his beloved son and then setting him on fire. However, when Abraham said, "We will come back to you," he was indicating that he had every intention of returning with Isaac, *alive*, from the mountains of Moriah. He was confessing his faith in God to raise Isaac from the dead by reconstituting his body back together from ashes.

It is hard to fathom how intense Abraham's faith must have been. He believed that God would do something that had never been witnessed by anyone. The New Testament writer of Hebrews confirms that Abraham had convinced himself and trusted that God would give him his son back: "Abraham reasoned that if Isaac died, God was able to bring him back to life again" (Hebrews 11:19, NLT).

People have often wished that they could have a deep and abiding faith in God, yet few are willing to give up something that they have worked intensely hard to attain so that they can head out in an unfamiliar direction simply because God was calling them to do it. It is a fact of nature that the older we get the more unwilling we desire a disruption to our regular routines. We become slaves to habit. Abraham, by the time God asked him to give up Isaac, was around one-hundred and thirty-three years old. He is proof that no matter how old we get we are still capable of accomplishing profound things for God. However, there must be a willingness to obey Him, even into the unfamiliar and uncomfortable. I believe that an ever abiding willingness to be flexible for God, a heart to embrace new possibilities, and an excitement to lay hold of new dreams and visions are secrets to longevity.

Abraham was a willing participant in the grand design of his Maker. After laying the wood upon Isaac's shoulder, he gathered the fire and the knife, turned his back to the two young male servants, and headed with Isaac toward Mount Moriah. Isaac then noted that they possessed wood and fire, but no lamb for the sacrifice. He asked his father why. He had, no doubt, participated in other worship ceremonies and would have known that a live lamb would have been necessary to honor Jehovah. The likelihood of finding a sheep in the wild was doubtful, so Isaac's curiosity was not unfounded. He knew well what was required for a sacrifice (Genesis 22:6-7).

Abraham's response to Isaac was a continuation of the faith he displayed when he informed the young men that he and Isaac (alive and well) would return together from Moriah. Abraham said, "My son, God will provide for Himself the lamb for a burnt offering" (Genesis 22:8, NKJV).

In addition to making a declarative faith statement, Abraham, perhaps unknowingly, was prophesying with impeccable precision and clarity the future coming of the Lamb of God, Jesus. As a matter of fact, when John saw Jesus coming to his baptism at the Jordan River, he proclaimed Him "the Lamb of God who takes away the sin of the world" (John 1:29)!

Abraham peered into the future and saw the Roman executioner's wooden crossbeam laid upon the shoulders of Jesus, and his brow bloodied by the wreath of two inch thorns driven into his head with cruelty, mockery and vicious cursing. God, indeed provided the lamb, and he was lit ablaze with the fire of His Father's wrath in order to appease His holy case against mankind. Like Isaac, Jesus humbled Himself, a lamb led to the slaughter, silent and willing, and walked the long road to the mount called the place of the skull, Golgotha. It was to Golgotha that Abraham had come with Isaac two-thousand years prior.

Abraham bound his son and laid him upon the altar he had fashioned with the wood and some loose stones. Isaac never whispered a peep as far as we know. He trusted his father, and so too would Jesus trust His Father to raise Him from the dead after making Himself an obedient and willing participant in His own Father's plans. Abraham lifted his knife high, and with a forceful uplifted arching motion—a movement designed to bring the knife down with enough force to instantly kill his son and splatter his blood on the altar of worship—drove the knife downward. Suddenly, with the knife inches from Isaac's neck, a voice from heaven seized him. His hand was miraculously stopped:

> But the Angel of the Lord called to him from heaven and said, "Abraham, Abraham!" So he said, "Here I am." And He said, "Do not lay your hand on the lad, or do anything to him; for now I know that you *fear God*, since you have not withheld your son, your only son, from Me" – Genesis 22:11-12, emphasis added

Abraham was likely faint from not breathing as he listened intently to God. Did he hear Him right? He had walked in obedience with God from that moment long ago when God told him to first leave his homeland. He never, as much as he could stand it, disobeyed one directive given to him. He trusted God through adversity and trial and difficulty. He once had to rescue Lot from captivity by regional warring factions, and he went a night without Sarah because a king, smitten by her beauty, had taken her away from him. He held onto God's promises, and while everyone around him worshipped gods they could feel, handle, touch, and see (wood, gold, silver and bronze), he instead followed a God that was unseen. He must have seemed a madman to those who knew him best. However, the skeptics could not deny the fruit of his life or deny his and Sarah's greatest miracle, the birth of Isaac. Yet, it wasn't until Moriah that God acknowledged that Abraham *feared Him*?

How could this be?

Up until then, he was known to God as a man of faith. God affirmed Abraham's faith by giving him Isaac. Additionally, God conferred the title of *righteousness* upon him, which attested to his unique standing with God. He had impressed and pleased God with the fidelity he showed toward Him, but it was not until he lifted his knife to slay Isaac that God declared Abraham a man who *feared Him* (Genesis 15:6).

We cannot let the magnitude of that moment slip by our understanding. For in that single event, there is entwined for us a very necessary truth: God will not trust His elite plans with those who regard Him as common or ordinary. Those that will do extraordinary things with Him will need to pass the *fear* test. Abraham passed.

God had to know that Abraham feared Him. There could be no question about it. God knows all things, and He certainly already knew what was in Abraham's heart. So why test him? He tested Abraham in order to see if there was anything in Abraham's life that he would fear more than Him. You see, had Abraham feared losing Isaac, he would have never been willing to let him go, and he would have eventually lost everything. The moment Abraham released Isaac as a willing sacrifice, Abraham expressed that he feared God alone. His obedience demonstrated where his fear was placed.

Additionally, God had to have a visible demonstration take place that would unleash a future drama that would be played out for the whole human race: the death, burial and resurrection of His Son. Isaac is called the *seed* of Abraham. When a seed is planted, it is only capable of producing after its own kind. Apple seeds do not grow to be watermelons. When Abraham sowed his *seed*, then God had to give him back the harvest of His very own Son, Jesus. God needed Abraham's cooperation to legally enter into human history (Genesis 21:12; Romans 9:7; Galatians 3:16; KJV).

Abraham gave his son and did not hold him back. God was under contractual obligation to give His. I would suggest that God could have never given Jesus if Abraham had never given Isaac. It was a tremendous risk, but then God knows that those who fear Him could be entrusted with the riskiest of endeavors. Abraham decreed that God would provide a lamb for a sacrifice, and God heard his words. He would do what Abraham had said if Abraham would follow through. Follow through, he did.

As well, this moment was not for Abraham alone, for there was a son watching his father's life of obedience and worship. We should not underestimate the impact that the events of that day on Moriah had upon Isaac. Our children are continually minding our connection or lack thereof to God. Abraham's actions and the ensuing words spoken to him, "Now I know that you fear God," left an indelible mark upon the young man, Isaac. So much was the impression made on him that he lived out his days in total reverence, respect, honor and regard for Jehovah. In fact, Isaac's son Jacob (Abraham's grandson), while taking an oath by the God of His fathers, called God "the fear of Isaac." Two generations after Abraham—and we can easily suggest every generation since—was impacted by the fear of God in his life. Parents would do well to follow Abraham's example, for their lives of their children depend on it (Genesis 31:42, 53).

The very instant Abraham heard God's words, he lifted up his eyes and saw that a ram had been caught by its horns a short distance away in a thicket of bushes and wild shrubbery. Typology was being played out in real time right before Abraham and Isaac's eyes. It was a shadow of what was to come, and Jesus would later be caught in the thicket of the mocker's thorns. Abraham took the ram which God had provided, and he and Isaac worshipped Him by giving it as a sacrificial offering upon the altar where Isaac had once lain. Abraham proclaimed the place to be forever known as *Jehovah-jireh*, which is interpreted to mean *the Lord sees*. God, upon Moriah, viewed mankind's deepest need and He provided. All of humanity owes Abraham a debt of gratitude for the *fear of God* that was operational in his life.

Immediately afterward, the Lord again confirmed His covenant with Abraham through Isaac, and then together they returned to the young men as Abraham had said they would, saddled their donkeys, and headed back to Sarah (Genesis 22:13-19).

Lessons from Abraham, the Great Intercessor

King David once wrote that "the eye of the Lord is upon them that fear Him," and this truth has been no more put on display than through the life journey of Abraham. God had followed him, His eye affixed upon His every move and location, from his first act of obedience to the day he obeyed in offering Isaac. Like a modern day homing-beacon or GPS-tracking-microchip, the fear of God draws the continual observation and monitoring of heaven, and Abraham never knew an instance when he was left without guidance and aid (Psalm 33:18).

I mentioned earlier in this chapter that Abraham was forced to part ways with his nephew Lot, whom he had taken into his care. Lot, fascinated by the natural beauty and lush terrain of the plains of Sodom and Gomorrah, left his uncle to herd his livestock in the desert region of Canaan.

Additionally, I referred to an instance when Abraham, along with his three-hundred and sixty-five personally trained servants, was compelled to rescue Lot after he was caught in the middle of a regional conflict and taken captive. Yet, there is another story involving Lot where we discover *Abraham the intercessor*.

Abraham's original call from the Lord required him to leave his country, family and father's house behind. He had to willingly surrender familiar surroundings and familiar people. He was told to let go of his homeland, siblings and extended family in order to follow God's plan. Abraham's brother Haran, Lot's father, had died prior to Abraham being called by God, and he and Sarah must have taken Lot into their family since they were without an heir at the time, but we cannot know for certain. However, we do know that by the time Abraham is instructed to leave everything and everyone, Lot was an adult and capable of making his own choices. The Lord was very clear; Abraham was *not* to bring any of his family on his faith journey (Genesis 11:27-31).

An all too often malady that afflicts God's children is the insistence on partially obeying Him. If partial obedience isn't bad enough, there is another problem common among believers that is just as problematic, and that is the compulsion to add on to His directives. These two challenges lie within our rational minds, but must be constantly put down so as to not create unnecessary life dilemmas. God gives very specific instructions for very specified reasons, and He does not always tell us what those reasons are, but we still must trust them. Adding on to His commands may come from a well-intentioned heart, but it is still regarded as rebellion.

When Abraham heard the Lord instruct him to leave his familiar surroundings, he obeyed. However, rather than trust the simplicity of leaving everything and everyone behind, including kinfolk, he allowed Lot to tag-along. When he departed with Sarah, the Bible tells us that "Lot went with him," which implies that Lot made a personal decision to follow them without compulsion. Instead of telling Lot that he ought to find his place among other family, Abraham *took* him as part of the caravan. That seemingly innocuous decision became a thorn in the side of Abraham and later in the side of the children of Israel. It is important that we do not add on to the Lord's commands (Genesis 12:4, 5, KJV).

While sitting in his tent entrance about ten miles west of the southwestern corner of the Dead Sea and *in the plains of Mamre*, Abraham was paid a visit from three mysterious men.

Seeing them, he ran outside of his tent, lifted his hand to block the blinding noonday sun, and recognized that it was the Lord. After falling upon his knees and bowing his head to the earth in worship, he begged the men to take refuge from the scorching heat and sunlight under a nearby tree. Abraham asked the Lord to relax awhile so that he could prepare refreshments and an afternoon meal. The Lord agreed to stay and dine with him (Genesis 18:1-8).

After spending a few hours conferring, the Lord suddenly fixed His attention and gaze southeast toward Sodom and Gomorrah. His business there was urgent, so He finished His conversation with Abraham and began His trek in that direction. It was a practice in those times for a gracious host to walk with his departing guests for a small fraction of their journey, so Abraham went along with the three men. As they walked together, the Lord discussed with the men that were with Him, while Abraham listened, whether or not He should tell Abraham what His business was for heading to the cities (Sodom and Gomorrah is a biblical designation for a region comprising of five cities which were each separated by only a few miles [Genesis 14:8]. They are also referred to as the *Cities of the Plain* in Genesis 13:12. Additionally, Sodom and Gomorrah were likely the largest, but were definitely the most wicked.) (Genesis 18:16-18).

The Lord knew that Abraham would become *a great and mighty nation*, and He also knew that Abraham could be trusted to "command his children and his household after him." Because of his consistent relationship with God and because he would be faithful to instruct his heritage to "keep the way of the Lord," God decided to tell him why He was headed to Sodom and Gomorrah: "Because the outcry against Sodom and Gomorrah is great, and because their sin is very grave. I will go down now and see whether they have done altogether according to the outcry against it that has come to Me; and if not, I will know" (Genesis 18:18-21).

The two angelic men went on ahead of the Lord, and Abraham was left standing before Him aghast. He knew that Lot was living in the city, and he also knew that God would find the place just as He stated, sin laced and reprobate.

Abraham and Lot's herdsmen couldn't get along, the land they shared could not sustain the two of them, Abraham had to deliver his nephew from certain death after he was taken hostage, and then Abraham found himself faced with the possibility that Lot was going to die in the overthrow of Sodom and Gomorrah. He no doubt blamed himself. Had he not allowed Lot to follow him when he left to pursue his destiny in God, he would've saved himself and Lot unnecessary grief on more than one occasion. Abraham knew that he would need to do something if Lot and his family were going to escape judgement.

He didn't hesitate:

And Abraham came near and said, "Would You also destroy the righteous with the wicked? Suppose there were fifty righteous within the city; would You also destroy the place and not spare it for the fifty righteous that were in it? Far be it from You to do such a thing as this, to slay the righteous with the wicked, so that the righteous should be as the wicked; far be it from You! Shall not the Judge of all the earth do right" (Genesis 18:23-25)?

Abraham's exchange with God presents us with 3 remarkable characteristics of intercession. Though not to be confused with the 7 steps I will present in the next chapter, these intercessory character qualities are no less valuable to our continued prayer success.

#1 – To Intercede Successfully, a Relationship with God Is Necessary:

> "Let us go right into the presence of God with sincere hearts fully trusting him." - Hebrews 10:22, NLT

While the first characteristic appears to be overly simplistic and obvious, it is vastly important. Notice that Genesis 18:23 says that Abraham "came near." This fascinating detail is indescribably glorious, because it describes a man who had great confidence in his relationship with God, a confidence acquired over many years. He knew that the Lord would not find him rude or obtrusive by getting up close and personal. Rather, Abraham was convinced that the Lord would find pleasure in his childlike, innocent and urgent approach.

There are many people who know about God, and while knowing *about* God isn't necessarily bad, *knowing* God is far better. Often, I am reminded of the difference in *knowing about* and *knowing* God while listening to people converse about celebrities. They quote facts, stats and news about their favorite actors or actresses as if they know them with personal intimacy. They know whom is dating whom, the names of their children, and who might be getting divorced and for what reasons. Sadly, while they can recite numerous details with specificity, they cannot claim to *know* the celebrities they gossip about. They can only claim to know some things *about* them.

It is important that we spend time in the Scriptures getting better aquatinted with the Lord, because it is there, in the Bible, where God has revealed Himself. Daily Bible reading is critical for personal growth. If we are going to know God, it will be through discovering Him in the Bible.

As important as studying the Word of God is, and while it is an essential aspect for gaining confidence within our relationship with our Creator, there is one thing that is more important than Bible reading. If all we know are facts, stats and information about God, without actually knowing Him, we will never pray with confidence. Bible reading will provide us with a trove of knowledge, but unless we have a relationship with God, through Jesus Christ, we will never really know Him. There is no other way to know God, and no other religious system that can truly reveal Him, except that we come to Him through fully trusting in Christ as both Lord and Savior (Acts 4:10-12; John 3:16-18).

Man was separated from God when he rebelled against Him in the Garden of Eden. The very instant man fell, God yearned for reconciliation with him, and so intense was the longing that He took the initiative upon Himself to repair and bridge the gulf. He provided the means whereby man would be reunited with Him, and He did it through Jesus' sacrificial death on the Cross. We can only know God through the completed work of the Cross, and any other attempt to satisfy our distance from Him will not work, no matter how hard we try. Jesus is the starting and finishing points of our relationship with God, and there is never going to be another person who will claim this role. To believe in alternate paths to God is to be led astray (Genesis 3; Hebrews 12:1, 2).

However, while most believers are aware of Christ's work to satisfy their distance from God, some still do not enjoy the confidence that is essential to boldly approaching Him as Abraham did. Paul, desiring to instill confidence in the Ephesians wrote to them and said, "You have been united with Christ Jesus. Once you were far away from God, **but now you have been brought near** to him through the blood of Christ" (Ephesians 2:13, NLT, emphasis added).

It is fascinating to consider that Abraham did not have the blood of Jesus to rely upon as we do today. Nevertheless, because he believed, God granted him intimacy, access and nearness. Jesus, in the Gospel of John, expressed that Abraham had seen His coming and was glad for it, and if we are going to find confident strength in our prayer life, then we too will need to spend more time rejoicing in what God has done for us in providing His Son. It is through Jesus that we can come near to our Father and pray for those we love, knowing that we have an audience with Him and that He longs to give us what we desire. Sadly, there are many people praying with little-to-no confidence.

Confidence is an interesting word. Its origin comes from the Latin prefix *con*, which means, *to have*, and the Latin word *fidere* which means, *to trust*. To be confident is to, *have trust*.

Abraham possessed a deep trust in God and in his relationship with Him. It showed in that he boldly approached God on behalf of Lot and the inhabitants of the city he dwelt in. We must place our confidence, our wholehearted trust, in Jesus, and know that through Him we can come to Father God and, with the same boldness that Abraham possessed, intercede for those whom we love.

#2 – To Intercede Successfully, the Intercessor Must Take Responsibility:

Often I hear Christian's bemoaning the evils of the United States of America, and while there is certainly plenty of unbiblical behavior to go around and plenty that should strike concern into our hearts, very rarely do I hear their complaints transition into an appeal for earnest prayer. The reason? They have not made a decision to own the problems they're making a fuss over. Being aloof and sanguine about the state of one's homeland is dangerous, but complaining about it and being unwilling to take ownership is far worse. If our prayers do not move us, they will not move God. When we won't identify with a problem so that it becomes personal to us, we will come up short of victory if we decide to pray at all.

Abraham took ownership and responsibility of Lot's citizenship in depraved Sodom. Also, he allowed the possible destruction of the rest of the populace to cause him grave concern, which in turn drove his appeal before God. He didn't want to see the cities and their inhabitants decimated, and he knew God could do it.

When things in our world are out of sight and out of mind, it is not possible for us to be moved by them. God will not expect us to care for something we do not know about. However, if we become aware of a terrible situation besetting our city, for example, and then regard it with little care and much apathy, it is nothing less than pitiful. Abraham did not allow unconcern to dull his heart and diminish his interest in what was happening nearby him. He feared what might happen if someone didn't intervene.

To be sure, our world is under extreme duress and suffering, and it is impossible to personally embody the oppression, heartbreak and pain of the entire globe. We aren't God, and even if we could carry the burdens of the planet, the sheer weight of them would crush us. However, if we witness a family member, close friend, colleague or neighborhood being buffeted by evil and remain silent in prayer, it is tantamount to sin. The oh-well-attitude or the if-it-does-not-affect-my-bottom-line-then-I-don't-care-mindset is certain to keep people and places bound by Satan.

The Old Testament book of Jonah reveals God as merciful and loving, even toward enemies of His chosen people. God told Jonah to go warn the people of Nineveh that unless they repented they would be destroyed. The people of Nineveh hated the nation of Israel and were known to publicly impale and hang their enemies on instruments that resembled large fishhooks. Jonah didn't want God to show them mercy, and he didn't want to be tortured. Jonah decided to reject God's plan and head in the opposite direction, but God forced him to change his mind after he commissioned a large fish to swallow him. When Jonah went to Nineveh and did as he was told, the people repented and God spared them. Jonah was angry and dejected because God had changed His mind and pardoned them, but God reminded Jonah that it was His prerogative to do so. God prefers mercy over judgement (Jonah 1-4; James 2:13).

God wanted Jonah to get involved with His sovereign desires, and it is safe to suggest that if Jonah had rejected God's call, Nineveh could not have been spared. God wanted a partner that felt what He felt and shared the responsibility of possibly saving a great city. When we allow God's heart to permeate ours, we will begin to sense His plans and purposes for those around us. I have often wondered how many people have been lost because someone didn't stand between God and them in intercession?

Many people believe that God will do whatever He wants and therefore excuse themselves from responsibility. They ask, "What is the point in getting involved or praying? God's gonna do whatever He wants to anyhow." Such thinking is wrongheaded.

We must understand that the lease (a lease may be understood as having the governance, authority or rule over a territory or property) of planet earth was given to Adam, and he represented every person that would come after him. Adam forfeited the lease to Satan, and therefore, everyone else lost the lease because of him. Satan became the god of this world. We can think of Satan as an evil landlord or, better yet, as a slum-lord. Jesus' Kingdom initiative was to reinvest the authority once surrendered back to His Body, the church. However, the total fulfillment of this won't be completely settled until Jesus takes His seat of authority and power in Jerusalem and rules earth for one thousand years. This will take place very soon, and at *that time,* the total will of God will be exacted without any hindrances from His enemies (Genesis 1:26-28; Genesis 3; 2 Corinthians 4:4; Luke 17:21; Acts 1:1-3; Revelation 20:1-6).

In the meantime, God needs agreement from mankind to intervene on their behalf. When Nineveh repented, God was able to intervene. Their repentance was their agreement with God. Without the repentance, they would have been wiped out, because just like Sodom, the cry of their sin invited His divine intervention, and *this is why the cries of intercession must be louder.*

In fact, when we pray, we allow God permission to act and get involved in varying circumstances. If this were not true, then why wouldn't God just fix all of the world's ills without people needing to pray or act? Also, if we pray, but cannot know if God will answer our petitions and intervene, then why pray at all? God most certainly hates things like children starving to death, sex trafficking, terrorism and governmental corruption, and He is not arbitrary, random or unpredictable.

Jesus came to put the lease back in to the hands of His church, and if Christians will not exact the authority of the Kingdom through intercession, then God won't get involved as much as He may want. God exacts His sovereign will by finding willing vessels through whom to work and pray forth His divine plans. Yet some people are left bereft of freedom and hope because someone else is being lazy, distracted and blasé. We must be willing to take responsibility like Abraham did.

#3 – Successful Intercession Requires Dogged Persistence:

In his exchange with God, Abraham asked Him to spare the cities of Sodom and Gomorrah, along with the other three cities that made up the cities of the plain, if fifty righteous people could be found in them. This is a remarkably low number considering that the total population of the five cities was probably high. The cities were, for their time, modern bustling metropolises and not any backwater-barely-inhabited places. In fact, excavations of burial grounds in the region uncovered 1.5 million skeletal remains and proved that the population was significant.[1]

The fact that Abraham only used fifty as his benchmark lends evidence to the fact that he was aware that the cities had become overgrown with wretchedness and evil. He knew that there weren't many that could be considered right in God's eyes. In addition, Abraham's request shows that he knew God was exceedingly *just, merciful* and *gracious.*

Abraham knew God was just and that God would never punish the righteous for the actions of the wicked. Abraham knew God was merciful and that God was inclined to withhold from men what they truly deserve due to His love for them. Abraham knew God was gracious and would be giving and generous, granting what mankind could never earn or deserve on their own.

Abraham started out by asking for the cities to be saved for the sake of fifty righteous people, but he continued to apply faith-pressure by lowering his benchmark until he reached a number he felt would be satisfactory to save his nephew Lot, his family, and the cities. Miraculously, Abraham's persistence paid off, and God agreed that if only ten righteous could be found among the depraved citizens then He would spare the rest.

We should never underestimate the power of what a few righteous people can do for God. It is amazing that Abraham believed the cities of the plain were worth saving for the sake of a handful of people. It is more amazing that God would agree.

---

[1] Aish.com, Biblical Archeology: Sodom and Gomorrah, Rabbi Leibel Reznick, http://www.aish.com/ci/sam/48931527.html

Dogged persistence in prayer like Abraham's is firmly grounded in the knowledge of God's character. A person remains prayerfully tenacious when they are confident and convinced that God is good and that He is not given to change. In fact, the successful intercessor should know that it is impossible for God to lie and that He never has lied or *plays* favorites among His people. God is faithful; He can be trusted. Abraham knew the Lord and so should we, and like any great relationship, vibrancy and richness comes over time and continual investment.

We should not give up on those we love and the places we dwell no matter how bad the circumstances look. There is always hope in God as long as faith in His Person is habitually maintained. He wants and longs to save the people and the places we love.

I know a woman whose family prayed for her for twenty-five years. During that time, she believed she was a homosexual. Her family persisted and wrestled for her soul until she finally found Christ and was miraculously saved. There were times she believed her family to be judgmental zealots when they tried to warn her. Nonetheless, they persisted in prayer for her, and they kept loving her. While driving alone in her car on a sunny afternoon, a Gospel song came on a secular R&B radio station, and she was forced off to the side of the road as the presence of God filled her vehicle. She wept uncontrollably as she repented for her sin, received Jesus, and felt His love wash over her. I had the personal honor of pastoring her for about eight years after her deliverance, and the double honor of being her nephew. It was my family that never gave up on her and never let go of God until He visited her.

I would love to share that Abraham's prayer saved Sodom and Gomorrah, but I cannot. Sadly, the cities were utterly destroyed just as God promised, but sadder yet, is the fact that there were not even ten righteous people residing among the whole population of the cities. In spite of the astounding devastation of the cities, Lot and his two daughters were saved, but not before his daughter's husbands, seduced by the immorality of their homeland, were killed with everyone else. As well, Lot's wife didn't want to let go of her *past* and was buried alive underneath a pile of fiery salt which had exploded up from the earth and then downward upon her.

The Apostle Peter, one of Jesus' original disciples and a New Testament writer, wrote that Lot's "righteous soul" was "vexed" continuously while living in Sodom and Gomorrah. God, by two angles, urgently ushered Lot and his family from the city. God mercifully saved them for Abraham's sake. During times when the temptation to doubt that our prayers are being effective, we must know that there is an invisible world being activated by our urgent petitions. Abraham's prayers saved His nephew through angelic intervention, and God will save our loved ones the same way (2 Peter 2:6-9).

Do not surrender the victory you long to possess for your family, friends and city. It is easy at times to give in to weariness, despair and spiritual fatigue. Instead, deepen your relationship with God by investing more time in it. Continue to be steadfast in taking ownership for those you desire to see liberated and remain confident and doggedly persistent before God. Fight the battle through to the end. You will win!

In the next chapter, I will assist you in how to pray with greater effectiveness, and I promise you results.

Chapter Nine
Seven Secret Steps to Successful Prayer

Sometimes, prayer is tough business. There is no doubt about it. Weariness, despair and frustration knock regularly on the door of the intercessor's heart begging to enter. Warding off these three evil intruders is a regular occurrence for the person who has learned to pray *through* until the victory is obtained. It is important that the intercessor not soon forget that God is totally, through His Son, invested in their success.

By keeping in mind the three characteristics of intercession discussed in the last chapter (A relationship with God, taking ownership and responsibility for the situation being prayed for, and dogged persistence), positive results are assured.

While it is true that these characteristics are needed for a positive outcome, it must be noted that their functionality is greatly dependent upon an overall *faith-filled* disposition and attitude. Manifold temptations to bring doubt will, at times, abound, and it is likely that there will be occasional fears to face. Therefore, a healthy, regular dose of the Word of God will be key to maintaining the faith it will take to win.

Romans 10:17 tell us that "Faith comes by hearing, and hearing by the word of God." Faith does not come to us through trials, sickness, life lessons or any other way. The delivery system deployed by God to transport faith is found contained in the words written in the Bible (More on this below under the 3rd step entitled *Stand*). Searching for promises to constantly think and meditate upon will be critical. For those uncomfortable or uneasy about searching the Bible for verses specific to a particular need, the internet is an invaluable resource. For example, a simple search of the phrase, *Bible promises for the protection of my family*, will return over two-million results.

Next, finding a prayer partner to regularly intercede with is another indispensable tool. Jesus encouraged us in the eighteenth chapter of Matthew that finding someone to "agree" with in prayer will work wonders:

> "Again I say to you that if two of you agree on earth concerning anything that they ask, it will be done for them by My Father in heaven." – Matthew 18:19, NKJV.

The word *"agree"* in the above verse comes from a Greek word that has the idea of a harmonious symphony of sounds. In a symphony, there are many different instruments with some of them playing at different intervals, pitches, sounds and volumes. Each instrument plays a part to complete the piece. If it is done right, the coming together of every separate and distinct section produces a sound that pleases the ear.

It is the same with prayer. Some people may pray loud while others pray soft, and some have a knack for eloquence while others pray in simple terms, but what is most important is that there is harmony. For example, if two people praying together have different expectations for the outcome of a prayer initiative, it is evidence that there is a lack of agreement, and their results will be hampered. They will not have success. Jesus promised prayer partners that if there is harmony of effort, then "it will be done for them of my Father in heaven."

Because of this, it is important that prayer partners share the same passion for the same outcome. Otherwise their efforts will be futile. I learned this lesson the hard way.

A dear friend and member of a church that I pastored fell severely ill. By the time I was able to get to him in the hospital, he was totally unconscious and on life support. When I arrived, I was informed that he had an internal defibrillator that was outdated and that his congenital heart condition had grown worse due to lack of continuing treatment. I also discovered at the hospital that he had made me his emergency contact, but not his power of attorney. He had no spouse or living relatives near him, so a brother that lived out of the state was left to make life and death decisions for him over phone calls with the medical staff. His situation was dire, so I immediately assembled our prayer team to go into around-the-clock prayer.

A few of days later, my friend died, and I was devastated.

Although we had the consolation of knowing that he was in heaven, his passing did not sit well with me. We were used to seeing miracles in our church, and his death didn't fit our standard of success. We once had witnessed a case of stage four ovarian cancer completely healed and marveled when the Lord gave a new heart to an infant whose mother was told the child would not live without a transplant. My friend's passing did not make sense, and I began to ask the Lord where I had gone wrong, and I soon found out.

In the instances where we had seen complete victory, I had instructed our prayer teams to pray in very specific ways. In fact, I had pleaded with any doubters to excuse themselves from our prayer chain—no one did. I maintained a steady stream of updates and continued to direct the course of the prayers, focusing our efforts with laser beam intensity. The battles were intense, but we prevailed every time.

When my friend fell ill, I had fallen under the poison of assumption and perhaps even some pride. I never doubted he would live and never considered that he could die, and I wrongly believed our prayer team would automatically, without persistent and consistent direction, know how to direct their prayers. I was wrong, and it cost my friend his life. I had failed to communicate what we were specifically agreeing about and gave vague and overly general guidelines.

I found out that some of our team thought he would die from the onset. Doubt had invaded our ranks. Fear melted some hearts, and others had been overcome by his appearance in the hospital: his body was swollen, his color was ashen, and a tube assisted him with breathing. Had I to do it over again, I would not have allowed anyone to pray at his bedside. I would have given better instructions with regularity, and I would have communicated with his brother before he settled on medical procedures. In the end, an attempt to get a scan of his heart disrupted his challenged breathing, and he died. I had failed to maintain total agreement among our team.

Our goal is to succeed, and while the primary focus of this chapter is on intercessory prayer for the lost and not the sick, the specific steps and dynamics will work the same for both.

Finally, and at the risk of being overly obvious, I want to reiterate and reemphasize that this book deals with the *fear of God* and its place in our lives. We have seen that famous men of the Bible, like King Solomon, Abraham and the Apostle Paul, understood that the fear of God should be as normal to a child of God as church attendance or Bible reading.

Throughout this book, I have made the case to the reader that the fear of God is a marvelous and glorious biblical truth that will open up a new world of experience with God. When the fear of God is embraced, we will begin to walk in the bounty of wisdom, and be invited by God to share in His elite strategies and plans for ourselves and mankind. Since it is not an uncommon practice for today's readers to jump around to various chapters that seem to be more interesting than others, I want to encourage a full embrace of the message of this book before entering into the forthcoming prayer strategies.

Before we ask God to work on the hearts of others, it is of the upmost importance that we be walking and living in an abiding reverence, regard and respect for God. This book will help in doing just that. By welcoming and allowing the Spirit of God to work upon our hearts to bring about a deeper commitment to holiness, faithfulness, purity and honor, we will be sure to pray from a confident footing.

We cannot allow Satan to whisper condemning words into our ears, and when we have unresolved sin in our lives or hatred and bitterness toward others, he is able to buffet us at his leisure. I am not suggesting that utter moral perfection is needed before God will hear us, because no one would be able to pray to Him. However, if we fail to forgive, to love others, and to rectify outstanding sin in our lives, then Satan gains a legal right through which he will continually accuse us before God and in our own thoughts.

Maintaining a faith-filled and confident disposition, finding a prayer partner to agree with, and personally walking in the fear of God is sure to be a strong foundation upon which to pray through the seven steps. At the end of the seven steps, I will provide a prayer guide/outline that shouldn't take more than three minutes to pray through. Quantity does not guarantee results as much as quality does. In fact, Jesus said, "And when you pray, do not use vain repetitions as the heathen do. For they think that they will be heard for their many words" (Matthew 6:7).

Military snipers are elite riflemen that take out hostile targets often from undetectable positions. They are a needed and necessary asset in combat situations, especially in eliminating opposing snipers or high level enemy operatives. Under special circumstances, a sniper will use a second person called a *spotter* who will assist him as a second pair of eyes for calculating distance, elevation, wind speed and direction, and discerning mirages. With a spotter's help, the sniper will be sure to hit his target when he pulls his trigger. The sniper could do all of these things himself—snipers start out as spotters—however, the smallest detail left unnoticed, like a slight cross-breeze for example, could render the shot useless. The extra eyes are crucial to a sniper's success.

When we pray, we should consider the Holy Spirit to be our spotter. His voice and guidance will help in making sure that we pray with accuracy. Some people have been led to believe that to pray effectively for a serious situation, prayer must be done for nonstop durations of time. While it is true that some circumstances require lengthy intervals of continuous intercession, it is not necessarily a rule for every situation. The Spirit of God can, with precise clarity, guide us in making sure that we hit our prayer targets with pinpoint accuracy. We do not always need many words, but what we do need is good information, and then the words *we do use* will do their intended work.

While we walk through the seven steps, allow the Holy Spirit to help bring greater understanding and insight to the truths presented. While the seven steps will help build a confident and knowledgeable prayer life, they are in no way intended to be the *corner* on intercessory prayer. The steps have been built over time with the aid of the Holy Spirit, yet they represent a small portion of the many wonderful revelations and teachings that are available to us today.

Additionally, I have not gained the seven steps from another author or Bible teacher, but that does not mean that they will not have similarities to other available teachings. In truth, I am an avid reader, and it is possible that books and articles I have read over the space of many years have greatly influenced these seven principles.

I Witnessed the Miracle of the Seven Steps

When I was given these steps, I had been in an extended season of prayer for a loved one. The person was in an unhealthy relationship, had a knowledge of God, but was living moderately compromised, was experiencing excessive mood swings—sometimes violent—and had grown unproductive and lethargic. I knew from years of experience that much of what I had witnessed was demonic in nature, so I began intensifying my prayer efforts. As I prayed, I saw momentary victories, but they were always short-lived.

One afternoon, while I poured my heart out before the Lord, He quieted me and began to deliver the steps. One-by-one they came in waves of wisdom, and I could barely keep up as I wrote the seven steps in my journal. I noticed that I had been praying through most of the steps over the years, but not in the order or with the focus that the Lord was revealing them to me at that moment. In a sense, they were not necessarily new to me, but He shined a new light *upon* them and showed me how to put the pieces together. I began that day to use the steps and the results were immediate.

Within the space of about twenty-one days, I saw the unhealthy relationship end completely, the mood swings ceased, the violent outbreaks stopped, and a repentant heart and total surrender to the Lord ensued. Within a few months, the person was fully involved in pursing their calling in God and had grown immeasurably.

Although, the results seem fantastical, I give my full assurance that they are not. Of course, this does not imply that the individual became a perfect person for whom growth in many areas was unnecessary, but the primary hindrance to their growth was removed, they were loosed from bondages, and made free to hear and sense God's leading for themselves. The transformation was, in a word, miraculous.

I have been reluctant to release these strategies, because I felt that they were simply a personal prayer method that had been given to me for personal use only. I didn't want to give them to anyone who hadn't labored over a loved one and heard the Lord for themselves, and I especially didn't want to share them if they weren't certain to work.

It wasn't that I didn't want to share; it is just that I didn't want to assume that God had given them to me to create a sermon out of them or to write a chapter in a book. I have always recoiled at the *look-what-God-gave-to-me* preachers that turn a personal revelation into a profit making venture.

However, because the results of the seven steps were so immediate and undeniable, I began to sense that I couldn't keep them to myself and that the Lord had allowed me to gain the knowledge over many years until He could trust me to faithfully steward them. As it stands, I have not preached one sermon about these seven steps and am only releasing them for the first time in this book. The reason for this is that the *fear of God* became a primary focus of one of the steps (I watched a sense of divine justice light upon my loved one), and when I felt the call to write this book, I knew that I could not exclude the prayer strategy from its volume.

It is my intention to support each step with multiple scriptural references, but I cannot include the verses in their entirety. Because of this, I hope that each reader will take the time to follow each verse to their specific location in the Bible and read through them. A couple of things will happen. First, an extraordinary assurance of faith will be established upon which each step can stand, and second, there will be greater comfort, familiarity and ease while perusing the Bible. For those already familiar with their Bible, many of the verses will be seen in a fresh and new light. In either case, for the Bible novice or the expert, an overall sense of empowerment and a reinvigorated and rejuvenated prayer life will be the outcome.

The Seven Steps:
Step 1: Repentance

> "If anyone sees his brother sinning a sin which does not lead to death, he will ask, and He will give him life for those who commit sin not leading to death. There is sin leading to death. I do not say that he should pray about that." - 1 John 5:16
>
> "Then He spoke a parable to them, that men always ought to pray and not lose heart, saying: 'There was in a certain city a judge who did not fear God nor regard man. Now there was a widow in that city; and she came to him, saying, 'Get justice for me from my adversary.'" - Luke 18:1-3

In the eighteenth chapter of Luke's Gospel, Jesus points out that God is a judge and that He presides over a heavenly court. God is the quintessential jurist. He hears cases, renders verdicts and dispenses with decrees. What He says is final. One of the finest ways we can regard prayer, in particular intercessory prayer, is to liken it to a person presenting a *case* in a court of law.

To understand the typical role of a judge in laymen's terms, think of a judge as a person who hears cases between two disagreeing parties. In a lawsuit, for example, a plaintiff (the party or person who brings a case against another) will seek financial damages by presenting in a court of law an argument against a defendant (the party or person being accused). After the case has been heard and the defendant has presented a counter argument, the judge will retire to consider all of the evidence.

The judge will weigh the plaintiff's claim against current laws as well as review settled and closed cases that are similar in nature to the one the plaintiff brought. Once a determination and verdict has been made by the judge, she will call the plaintiff and defendant back into her court, and she will issue her final say on the case. If the outcome is unsatisfactory to either the plaintiff or the defendant, the case may be appealed, and another court may decide to take up the case, or a judge or judges can exercise their discretion and simply throw out the case.

The woman in Luke 18 was being viciously harangued by an adversary, so she took her case to the court and begged for action. She was likely seeking a court enforced restraining order against the harassing party. The judge was initially reluctant to regard her case, but after the woman persisted and pressed her case before the court, the judge ordered action on her behalf.

Jesus used the parable to explain that, unlike the human judge, God is a just and fair Judge. He will always hear the cases that His people bring before Him, and He will not turn them away. Additionally, Jesus showed us that God will act swiftly to avenge His people against their adversaries, but we cannot be afraid of persistently pressing our cases before Him.

When a person brings a case before a court of law against another person, they are in essence acting as an *accuser*. Judges must do their very best to determine if accusations that are brought before them are founded. It is the job of the defendant's legal team to provide counter-evidence to a judge and, in some cases, will counter sue the plaintiff and bring accusations against them. Judges have the responsibility of sifting through piles of testimony in each case they hear and must make sure to judge each case in a manner that is untainted by personal agendas.

Honest and fair judges are essential in maintaining law and order, and societies cannot thrive if their judges are given to taking bribes or payoffs. While the judge in Jesus' parable is unjust, He tells us that we can count on God being an impartial and a completely righteous judge.

When the woman in Jesus' parable brought her case before the judge, she was *accusing* another person of being an oppressive adversary. In Scripture, Satan is referred to as an *adversary* and an *accuser*. These terms are important when we consider where he brings his accusations against us. The final book of the Bible, Revelation, tells us that Satan *accuses* us before God, and I believe he does this in God's courthouse in heaven. This is an astounding reality to consider. While some may disagree, there is ample evidence to suggest that Satan's use of accusations against us is to seek legal grounds upon which he may buffet us (Luke 18:1-8; Job 1:65-12; 2:1-8; 1 Peter 5:8; Revelation 12:10).

In other words, Satan seeks to deceive us into sin on many different levels, because apart from us allowing him to, he cannot touch us, and he knows it. Since the Bible defines sin as "the transgression of the law," it is obvious that Satan uses sin as a basis upon which he can afflict and bind people with many types of bondages. All too often, we find ourselves vigorously praying for a loved one while making very little headway. The reason for this may be that Satan has a binding legal case against the person we are praying for through their words, continued sin, and acts of rebellion. His accusations are not made up, and it is a mistake to assume that they are. We must accurately identify the sin patterns and negative confessions (more on this in a later step) of the person for whom we pray, and we must bring a counter case before heaven's court (1John 5:18; 3:4).

Repentance is a crucial element in interceding for another person. I am amazed that very few Christians understand that they can present a person before God and repent for them as if the person were repenting before God themselves. Jesus was known for remitting the sins of people while they never actually asked to be forgiven. In fact, He was attacked for exercising His executive privilege to remit sins, and He has actually extended this same grace to His Body on earth.

The greater our authority over a person and the closer the relationship, the more powerfully this works. Parents have a unique authority over their children and grandchildren, and spouses have a special prayer authority over the other spouse. Pastors have authority over their flocks. When we understand this and grasp the implications of Jesus' Cross and it's universal and eternal legal impact upon us, we will pray in a new light and with fresh zeal (1 John 5:16; Matthew 9:2-6; Luke 7:47-48; 1 Corinthians 7:4, 14; Isaiah 53).

When you bring your loved one before the Lord, it is important to bring every single sinful act up before God and then repent for it. This is where knowledge of the Bible becomes critical, because if there is the slightest ignorance or slight violation of the Word of God, then there will likely only be moderate victory. Additionally, quieting oneself and simply asking the Holy Spirit to reveal hidden things is also an essential element in seeing that Satan loses his legal grip on the person we are praying for.

Here is a list of things, albeit not exhaustive, that must absolutely be repented of:

- Habitual lying, cheating or stealing
- Laziness and sloth
- Habitual drunkenness and drug use of every kind, including legalized drugs
- Disrespect and dishonor of parents
- Sexual promiscuity and all sex outside of the covenant of marriage
- Dabbling in or practicing witchcraft, occultism and dark arts
- Practicing Eastern mysticism or the embracing of false religions
- Wrath, rage, irrational or erratic behavior
- Self-deprecating words like, "I hate myself," or "I wish I were dead" et al

When the person being prayed for finally comes to the saving faith found freely in Christ, all of the above actions will be washed away from their record, and Satan will no longer have anything to accuse them with. However, the goal of repenting on behalf of those we are praying for is to render Satan's access to them ineffective. Without repenting for them, we cannot provide them with a clear mind and heart to hear the call of God and yield to the Hound of Heaven. We must counter Satan's legal claims by reminding the Father, with the same force and vigor that Satan uses, that He sent His Son to die for the person we are interceding for. Reminding God of His mercy will always garner His attention (Isaiah 43:25-28; 2 Peter 3:9).

Moreover, if the person being prayed for is someone that has known the Lord but then walked away, they too will need to personally repent. In the meantime, their sins will need to be repented of by the intercessor. It is true that they may not have lost their place in heaven while they are in a backslidden condition, but if they continue in their folly, they may be visiting it sooner than expected. Satan takes his assaults on God's children very seriously, and we as intercessors must take our position before God as we learned Abraham did (chapter 8) and neutralize Satan's access to them. Their sin may not send them to hell, but it will give Satan a legal point of entry into their lives (Romans 6:23; Genesis 18:22-23).

This first step cannot and should not be taken lightly, because without success here, the rest of the steps will not produce as powerfully as they would have otherwise. Jesus understood the importance of keeping the door shut on Satan and not allowing him any claim upon Him when he said, "The ruler of this world is coming, and he has nothing in Me" (John 14:30).

Notice a couple of things: First, Jesus acknowledges that Satan is the *ruler* of this world and admitted that he has maintained a legal standing as a governor over planet earth and its residents. Adam's forfeiture allowed this to happen, yet salvation through Christ relinquishes Satan's legal claim on believers. Secondly, Satan didn't have a legal accusation against Jesus that could gain him domination over Jesus' life (John 14:30).

There is an additional repentance step that should not be overlooked by the intercessor. After repenting for the sins and negative words of the person they are praying for, the intercessor should consider whether or not any of his or her own words or actions have given Satan access to the person for whom they pray.

When I was praying for my loved one, I had to consider my own words and actions, and I was surprised to find that I had encouraged a legal claim upon them. I had said and done things that seemed, at the time, just to be an angry outburst or an innocent decision, but I discovered that every seed sown will reap a harvest, and that there was no circumventing it (Galatians 6:7-8).

Repenting and renouncing previous actions is a powerful weed killer to render Satan's legal claims against the person being prayed for null and void. A wife who is interceding for her husband to leave an adulterous relationship cannot spend the week calling him a "bum and a loser" and expect her prayers to be effective, because he will likely continue being a "bum and a loser." Likewise, a parent cannot call their teenage child a "lazy-good-for-nothing" and think that their prayers are going to produce a diligent and respectable child, because the seeds being planted with their words can only produce what they presently are: a lazy-good-for-nothing.

This may be hard to read, but a failure to own responsibility, when needed, in the rebellion and wayward lives of those being prayed for will only produce limited results. Parents will need to repent if there has not been harmony and agreement in the marriage, because an out of order household will produce rebellious children. Husbands that send their wives off to church while they go fishing every week and refuse to submit to spiritual authority, such as his pastor and elders, can expect their kids, at some point, to stop obeying and yielding to them. They have personally sowed the seeds of their child's rebellion.

Divorce is a very tender topic, especially in Christian circles, and while I do not come from a theological persuasion that suggests that divorce disqualifies a person from Christian service or receiving the sacraments, I am convinced it opens up a host of problems that kids of divorce must contend with. A recent study by The Public Religion Research Institute revealed that *millennial's*—those born between 1982 and 2002—whose parents divorced at some point in their adolescence have "grown up to be adults with no religion."[2]

It is true that people divorce for various reasons, which are deeply personal and usually painful. There is not a person who hates divorce more than those who have had to endure it. No one should stay in a marriage where there is abuse, abandonment or adultery. However, those who follow Christ and who are intent on seeing their child or children surrendered to God, must at least consider that their divorce allowed Satan an opportunity to place a spirit of rebellion upon their kids, which has kept them from church and from God. Rejecting this as a possibility for why intercession seems weak and ineffective will likely lead to continued prayer failures.

The Bible reveals that whole territories have fallen under economic blight and depression because of the deeds of previous

---

[2] Zauzmer, Julie, *How decades of divorce helped erode religion* (The Washington Post, https://www.washingtonpost.com/news/acts-of-faith/wp/2016/09/27/how-decades-of-divorce-helped-erode-religion/. Accessed 27 October 2016).

leadership, so it is not impossible to believe that families have had the same challenges because of the actions of grand-ancestors or parents (2 Samuel 21:1).

Please consider whether or not all or some of these actions will need to be repented of while praying for your loved one (Again, the list is non-exhaustive):

- Divorce
- Abandonment, abuse or adultery
- Word curses, such as "You're stupid, an idiot, ugly, a liar," or "You're just like uncle Bill; he was a lazy drunk, and you'll always be too," or "You treat me just like my dad did my mom," or "I never loved you and don't know why we ever married!"
- Alcohol or drug abuse, especially during a child's formidable years
- Not attending church or submitting to the authority of church pastors or elders (Hebrews 10:25-26)
- Raising children in a perfectionist, graceless or rigid environment where failure was frowned down upon and mistakes were unwelcome
- Not telling children that they are loved
- Withholding affection from a spouse or child when angry
- Habitual quarreling and arguing among spouses in the presence of children
- Gossip, backbiting or questioning authority figures, especially in the presence of children, which will foster a rebellious spirit

Step 2: Petition

> "Now this is the confidence that we have in Him, that if we ask anything according to His will, He hears us. And if we know that He hears us, whatever we ask, we know that we have the petitions that we have asked of Him." - 1 John 5:14-15
>
> "Be anxious for nothing, but in everything by prayer and supplication, with thanksgiving, let your requests be made known to God." - Philippians 4:6

A petition is simply a request. When we intercede for another person, we are requisitioning or petitioning the high court of heaven to intervene in their life. This may seem overly simple, but where many people fall short is that their petitions are vague and unfocused. *When interceding, we must state our petitions in the clearest terms possible.* In other words, the intercessor must say specifically and clearly what it is they desire the Lord to do. They must know what they want!

A request may be adjusted, adding additional details as facts are made available by the Holy Spirit, but there must be a focused and precise petition that is made daily until victory is obtained. *Therefore, writing down the request is essential.*

Without putting pen to paper, there is likely going to be prayer that resembles what it would be like trying to hit a bullseye one hundred meters away with a shotgun rather than a long range rifle. Also, writing the petition out acts as a sort of contract between the intercessor and God. There is something divine about specifying a need upon a sheet of paper (Habakkuk 2:2).

As well, if a person doesn't know what they want, how should they expect God to know for them? Of course, God is omniscient, and Jesus did say that the Father knows everything that we "need" before we ask, but He was emphasizing the wrongheadedness in using many words simply to meet a preconceived volume requirement instead of praying specifically. While it is true that there are times that we are at a loss for words, and we do not know how to specifically pray, the Bible does point out that there are many instances where we should pray unambiguously. In fact, Jesus was not suggesting that we can leave our prayers vague and shallow and then wait upon God to work out the rest of the details. He was reminding us that our relationship with God is what precedes our petitions being granted, and answers are never based on how long we pray and neither is it found in how many words we use. Our confidence for answered prayers rests in the knowledge of our Heavenly Father's love for us (Matthew 6:7, 8; Romans 8:26).

If we didn't need to ask God and could simply let Him do whatever He wants, then why pray for anything at all? I have had people tell me that they don't ask God for anything because He already knows what they need, but I have also observed that these same people are usually the most miserable people I know. Jesus tells us to ask in more places than He tells us not to, and He said that answered prayer would bring joyful satisfaction (Mathew 7:7-11, 18:19, 21:22; John 14:13-14, 15:7, 15:16, 16:23-26).

While Jesus was traveling with His disciples, a blind beggar called out to Him for mercy. As Jesus' entourage moved away from the blind man, he shouted out even louder, so Jesus stopped and asked that the man be brought to Him. When the man got close enough for Jesus to speak to him, Jesus asked Him what he wanted.

It doesn't take an advanced degree in the Bible to know what a blind man who was a vagrant and begging for mercy truly wants. A blind man would desire sight more than anything else, but Jesus didn't do a single thing for him until He was asked clearly and specifically by the blind man. Suppose he would've asked for help in getting a job or for money. Jesus would have honored his faith as he expressed it in his request, not as he may have assumed Jesus supposed it. Jesus knew the man wanted sight, but He wanted to know if the man knew that he needed sight over all of the other possible requests (Mark 10:46-52).

I have heard women begging God to save their husbands from their sin-laced lives, because they yearned for a good marriage after years of suffering through quarrels and suspicion. I have also heard them plead with God so that their children would have a dad that spent time with them. While I never fault a desperate woman for praying in such a manner, none of those reasons are really what the woman wants and what she should be pleading with God for. The real prayer should be focused on the man coming into a right relationship with God and to be delivered from certain eternal destruction should he die. The most earnest appeal needs to be spent reminding the Lord that He does not desire one man to perish, and that would include her husband. The woman should spend the majority of her time interceding for her husband to be saved, because His life will find meaning and purpose only in Christ, not in sinful pleasures. When He makes peace with God, all of her other desires will be satisfied.

It goes without saying that a man with sight can go get gainful employment and earn some money on his own. Jesus knew this well, but He was not going to tell the man how to pray. The blind man had to know what he wanted and so must every intercessor.

Petition God in the clearest terms possible. Know what you want God to do, state it clearly, and write it down.

Step 3: Stand

> "So then faith comes by hearing, and hearing by the word of God." – Romans 10:17
>
> "Let us hold fast the profession of our faith without wavering; (for he is faithful that promised;)" – Hebrews 10:23, KJV
>
> "This book of the law shall not depart out of thy mouth; but thou shalt meditate therein day and night, that thou mayest observe to do according to all that is written therein: for then thou shalt make thy way prosperous, and then thou shalt have good success." – Joshua 1:9, KJV

Faith begins where the will of God is known. The will of God is found in the Word of God, the Bible. There can be no confidence in prayer without knowing what the will of God is. Whatever we are interceding for, it is imperative that we *stand upon definite promises from the Word of God specifically regarding our petition.*

When I was praying for my loved one, I took a daily stand on at least 13 different verse locations representing about 45 verses. I first repented, then I made a very clear petition which I had written out, and then I leveraged God's promises. I made it a point to remind the Lord of what He had promised me regarding the person for whom I was praying, and as I shared above, God did not disappoint me (Isaiah 43:26).

When we pray according to the revealed will of God, we do not have to *wish* for God to hear us, but we can *know* for certain that He does. In a sense, we are not relying on our personal faith to get the job done, but rather on His faith inside of us. Above, I shared Romans 10:17 which states that "faith comes by hearing and hearing by the word of God." I love words, and I have always imagined them as containers that carry different things. Words can carry hate, fear, doubt, love, encouragement or many other things. God's Words carry and deliver faith, and when we receive His Word into our hearts, His faith becomes our own.

When I was a young Christian, I spent many hours shouting at the devil until my throat was raw. God was always so patient and gracious to me, but eventually, I learned that I was praying from the wrong position. I learned that Satan had been cast down to earth and that he and his hoards dwell in the unseen realm all around us. This is the same place that angels function. However, God does not want us to pray from the earth up, but from heaven down. He wants us to intercede from our position in His Son and seated at His right hand. From this fixed and firm position, we do not need to scream and holler or necessarily address the devil. There are some cases where this is needed, and we will look at it in step 5, but what we must do is activate the Word of God and set

God's Kingdom loose to finish the job. His Word will work if we will turn it loose from our heart and lips (Luke 10:18; Revelation 12:10; Ephesians 2:6; Colossians 3:1-3).

The practice of speaking the Word of God—some call it confession—is as old as Abraham. We've already learned in chapter 8 that God imbedded a *faith* confession into Abraham's very name by changing it from Abram to Abraham. When any one asked Abraham his name, he was *confessing* that he was the *father of many nations*.

Additionally, at one of Israel's most dramatic transitions of power when God handed national leadership over to Moses' successor Joshua, He told Joshua to keep the Word of God in His mouth. By doing this, God promised him success and prosperity.

However, in recent years, some have criticized *confessing* the Word of God as being New Age. As well, others have tied it to branches and movements within Christianity that have sadly bent towards various degrees of abuse and misuse, such as the so-called Prosperity Gospel Movement. While it is not my aim in this book to defend the legitimacy of any group of ministers and their message (or condemn them), I have to stress that is still unwise to throw the baby out with the bath water. Jesus remains the "High Priest of the confession…of our faith" (Hebrews 3:1, 4:14, 10:23).

Most know about the confession of sin, but few know that there is also a *confession of faith*. A confession of faith is, first and foremost, an affirmation of our allegiance to Christ and His Cross, but it does not end there. If it only ended at the confession of Christ's lordship, then that would be plenty, but that is only the doorway into this marvelous truth. We are charged by God to make as many faith confessions as the Word of God permits.

The duty and function of the High Priest is to be a mediator between man and God. In the Old Testament, their primary duty consisted of receiving the offerings of the people and to present the blood of a pure sacrife once a year in the Holiest of Holies on Yom Kippur, the Day of Atonement. They, the High Priests, made intercession for Israel as an intermediary (Exodus 28:1; Numbers 18:7, 27:21; Leviticus 4:3-21, 16:14-15, 21:6-8; Hebrews 9:1-28).

In like manner, Jesus presented His own blood as our atoning sacrifice into the very throne room of God in heaven. He is the New Testament equivalent, but with greater authority, of the Old Testament High Priest. One of the functions of Jesus' High Priestly ministry is that He makes intercession for us. That's right; Jesus prays for us. In fact, He is tireless with the task of prayer. It would be unwise to assume that since Jesus is praying for us that it excludes our need to pray for ourselves, because Jesus is actually charged as the "High Priest of our confession" with praying what *we pray* for ourselves and others. In essence, He aligns Himself with our faith declarations we make through prayer (Hebrews 7:25; ch.9).

It is essential to couple our intercessions with scriptural declarations that guarantee that Jesus will take our prayers, as our chief heavenly advocate, before the throne of God and enforce a *restraining order* upon the enemy. In the prayer outline that I provide at the end of this chapter, I will make it as scripturally tight as possible. Since we will be focusing our prayers for those who have walked away from God or who have never known Him, the outline will already include a sound faith declaration. Additionally,

I will provide some supplemental scriptural references that will prove helpful if greater specificity is desired.

Step 4: Bind

> "Assuredly, I say to you, whatever you bind on earth will be bound in heaven." - Matthew 18:18
>
> "The tongue can bring death or life; those who love to talk will reap the consequences." - Proverbs 18:20, NLT

By this point in the 7 step intercessory prayer process, the person being prayed for is nearly unencumbered (Step 5 will complete this process). The legal basis for Satan's control over them has been neutralized. God, by this stage in the prayer steps, is mightily at work aligning various unseen things to bring about total victory. Repentance, a clearly stated written petition and the verification of the Word of God to support the request, has left the enemy frustrated. However, the person being prayed for cannot remain in a vacuous state. Aristotle once said that "nature abhors a vacuum." He meant that something left empty will be filled by something else. We must bind the person to the will of God concerning salvation, faith, grace, mercy and every other good thing found in the Word of God.

When Israel's leader, Moses, was planning the nation's transition of power, he gave them a choice between *life and death and blessing and cursing*. He said that their choice would directly impact and influence their children. The same is true today. Parents are responsible for choosing life and blessing for their children, and one spouse can do the same for the other (Deuteronomy 30:19).

The word "bind" in Matthew 18:18 literally means to *tie*. Jesus was delegating a spiritual authority to His people which granted the right to make prayer decrees that He promised heaven would endorse. If we choose to bind those whom we are praying for to the mercy, love, grace or fear of God, Jesus says it will be done. This is vital when we understand that Satan would prefer that people be bound to rebellion, pride, selfishness and evil conduct.

So often, people have asked me why they only witness temporary victories for the people they intercede for, and when I ask them to share with me how they have been praying, I realize that a major part of their failure is tied to a misunderstanding of how to properly *bind*.

Additionally, I have heard people, in prayer, *binding* the devil. I am not sure where this teaching came from, but I have heard the phrase, "I bind you devil," as a common prayer refrain among charismatics. I am well aware that Jesus said that if a strongman's house is to be plundered, then the strongman would need to be bound, but He did not specify how the strongman was to be bound. He had just concluded casting a demon out of an individual, and His teaching on binding the strongman followed. It may be true that binding Satan in prayer is an entirely acceptable practice, but another practice of binding that must never be neglected has to do with speaking the Word of God over those we are praying for (Matthew 12:22-37).

A careful observation of people's lives and decisions will prove how often people are living out the expectations and words of key authority figures. It is sad to say, but many children have repeated the sinful cycles of a parent, not only through nurture, but because the other parent said they would end up being like the other. Words are potent, and while I do not have time to unfold the majestic truth behind the power of words, I will say that those who do not believe that their words can carry life and death are at a marked prayer disadvantage. There is little to lose in trusting what I am presenting here, especially because I have witnessed the outworking of it in real time.

One more thing ought to be shared before we proceed to the fifth step, and that is that all of these steps are assuming verbal prayer as opposed to contemplative, meditative prayer. I am well aware that some Christian circles emphasize simply thinking one's prayers, but I find this to be biblically inaccurate, especially for intercession. I do not mean to demean anyone's sensibilities or intelligence, but I need to be clear that prayer which is spoken out loud is an absolute must for the 7 steps to be successful. There is no record of Jesus ever teaching or ever praying in a manner that didn't use or emphasize speaking the prayers out loud. We should not allow ourselves to be driven by traditions when they are not in correspondence with Jesus' practice or His instruction on a given subject.

Step 5: Sever

"And whatever you loose on earth will be loosed in heaven." - Matthew 18:18

> "So it will be at the end of the age. The angels will come forth, separate the wicked from among the just." - Matthew 13:49

Severing is the opposite of tying to bind. This is both apparent and obvious. Step 5 requires that we sever the person for whom we are praying from any and all foul workings of the enemy, Satan, his demons, or his agents that work in and through men and women or in the person themselves.

An honest observation and assessment of steps 4 and 5 would require us to ask why wouldn't severing or loosening someone from evil precede tying them to good and not the other way around? My only answer for this question is that this is how the steps were given to me. Since these steps are not to be taken as complete authority or absolute truth, I would not be uncomfortable if the reader decided to swap out steps four and five. However, I will emphasize once again that I have used these steps in their presented order and have seen them work wonders.

Often, and most likely consistently, the person we are interceding for is wrapped up in relationships, friendships, allegiances, alliances and associations that are helping to facilitate a rebellious life. These relationships come in different types of packages. Some are romantic, while others are business related, and some are as simple as lifelong friendships. Yet, and it is sad to say, there is a direct corollary between a person's company and the level of their spirituality.

Birds of a feather flock together.

When I was praying for my loved one, I knew I was contending with an unhealthy relationship that they were continuously engaging in. In fact, the relationship was unhealthy for both my loved one and the other person. They had simply become toxic to each other, and they were both driving the other to react and behave in ways that was not in line with the Lord's desires. No amount of pleading, prodding or begging seemed to assist in severing the relationship. However, when the Lord gave me this prayer strategy, the results were almost immediate. Decisions to abstain from contacting one another were made, phone numbers and social media accounts were blocked, and advice was sought out, received and implemented.

It is not always necessary to identify the unhealthy relationship. Sometimes, it may be that the relationship is virtual, such as pornography, roll-playing games, or online gaming. As well, the relationship may seem innocuous and innocent. By making a simple generalized declaration that severs the evil bondages and influences from a person, whatever they may be, unhealthy and ungodly patterns of behavior will be mitigated.

In rare cases, but important to mention nonetheless, a person may be victimized by strong demonic ties due to vows taken during occult practices. Sometimes an ancestor's involvement in the occult may be the root issue impeding a release from rebellion. These ties, often in the form of vows, will need to loosened from the person being prayed for.

In fact, Jesus warned about taking vows and said that some vows proceed from the evil one. How often have I cringed when hearing a young person using the common American colloquial: "I swear on everything." While this expression may be meant to convey one's seriousness and truthfulness, it is actually a vow that Satan will exploit. Other vows are even more powerful while appearing to be innocent common cultural expressions (Matthew 5:33-37).

I have a relative who has been continuously beset by stomach and bowel issues while being of an age that would normally assume overall health. No amount of praying has alleviated her discomfort and unease, and doctors have been unsuccessful in providing a treatment plan that eliminates the problem permanently. One afternoon at a family gathering, I heard her say at least a few times, "That just tears me up inside." Without realizing it, she had been giving permission for her affliction through her own words. She was cursing herself and binding herself to sickness. I attempted to speak to her about what I believed was hindering her from being healed, but she rejected me, choosing rather to believe that her words were nothing more than harmless figures of speech. Needless to say, she has still yet to find relief from her ailments.

Through the aid and guidance of the Holy Spirit, things will be brought to our attention. However, we must be willing to listen to Him during the intercessory process. He is sure to point out, very specifically and accurately, the things that should be loosened from the people that we are praying for.

This step should not be taken lightly, and it is certain to expedite the deliverance of our loved ones.

Step 6: Release the Power of the Holy Spirit

> "And when He has come, He will convict the world of sin, and of righteousness, and of judgement." – John 16:8

> "Then He said unto me, Prophesy unto the wind, prophesy, son of man, and say to the wind, 'Thus says the Lord God: Come from the four winds, O breath, and breathe on these slain, that they may live.'" – Ezekiel 37:9, KJV

When the Lord gave me step number six, I trembled. Frankly, I questioned whether or not I had heard Him correctly. I knew already that the Spirit of God was actively involved in bringing men and women to Christ. I, however, was not completely aware that intercessors could partner with Him in His work. What a joy it was to my soul to learn that the Holy Spirit takes great delight in working out the eternal purposes of the Father and the Son, together, along with us.

In the thirty-seventh chapter of Ezekiel, God showed Ezekiel, in a vision, a valley that was filled with an innumerable number of bones. The bones had been sun-scorched and bleached from lying in the desert valley for a very long time. Any meat and skin that used to be upon the bones had long before been picked over by ravenous birds and other flesh-eating vermin. The bones were disjointed, disconnected and dispersed throughout the valley. The situation that God presented before Ezekiel was hopeless and bleak.

While the chapter speaks of the dispersed House of Israel and their future ingathering and replanting in the Holy Land, it also tells of the common affliction of mankind and the ravages of what happens when life is lived in sin outside of the will of God. Man without God is hopeless. God's solution to the problem in the Valley of Dry Bones is an interesting one: it is Ezekiel's mouth. God told Ezekiel to prophesy.

When people hear the word *"prophesy,"* they rightly assume it means future-telling. However, to prophesy in its simplest definition is to *release* destiny into a situation or circumstance with God-words. Ezekiel was charged with releasing a prophetic declaration to cause the bones to be joined together and for muscle and skin to return as well. God basically told him to reverse years of destitution with a prophetic declaration. Often, the child of God feels completely hopeless in their circumstances, not realizing that God has given them the solution with the use of their mouth.

After Ezekiel made his initial decree, the bones came rattling back together, and the flesh returned as well, but the bodies were still lifeless. God, again, commanded Ezekiel to prophesy, but this time, He told him to command the *four winds* to *breathe* on the lifeless bodies. It was a rather odd command since *winds* do not *breathe*, but this was no common *wind* and no ordinary *breath*.

In both the Old and New Testament, the words that are normally translated into the English word "spirit*"* (or "ghost," depending on the translation) comes from a Hebrew or Greek word that can also be easily translated as *wind* or *breath*. The Holy Spirit, therefore, is the Holy Breath or Holy Wind of God. There are other descriptive words used to describe the Holy Spirit and His operation, such as fire and water. The Holy Spirit Himself is

God, and the Holy Breath represents only one of His many manifestations.

Consider these remarkable verses of Scripture:

> "Knowing this first, that no prophecy of Scripture is of any private interpretation, for prophecy never came by the will of man, but holy men of God spoke as they were moved by the Holy Spirit." – 1 Peter 1:20, 21
>
> "All Scripture is given by inspiration of God." – 2 Timothy 3:16

Notice that it was the Holy Spirit being active upon the holy men of old that brought forth prophecy and Scripture. The Bible itself refutes the claim that men thought up the idea of writing the Bible, stating that the *will of man* had nothing to do with its origin and compilation. Besides, since the Bible was written over a fifteen-hundred-year span with over forty writers, such a feat would have been impossible to accomplish, especially since it is harmonious and complete in its message.

The Bible was given by what Paul calls *inspiration*. In fact, the entire phrase, *"given by inspiration of God,"* comes from one Greek compound word: *theopneustos*. The word means *God-breathed*. In other words, God breathed on men by the power of the blessed Holy Spirit, and they wrote the Holy Scriptures and prophesied.

The wind that God spoke of was the Holy Spirit, and it would be His divine breath that would give life and animation to the lifeless, numberless multitudes that stood before Ezekiel. Dead things must come alive when the Spirit of God is operative. God's command to Ezekiel was for him to *say to the breath* to *come from the four winds*. In other words, he was to speak to the Holy Spirit, and the Holy Spirit would graciously respond to him. It was a similar command that God had given to me, and it was the reason why I trembled.

Initially, I was reluctant to obey. It was hard for me to think of myself in the same company of the beloved prophet Ezekiel, and furthermore, who was I to speak to the Holy Spirit, God Almighty? Why should He respond and move on my decree?

As I pondered these questions, a flood of biblical passages began to wash over me. The passage from Ezekiel was one of them that lighted upon my heart and mind. I also saw that the Holy Spirit was instrumental in the recreation of the earth when it had been in a chaotic and catastrophic condition. It was dark and void of life and light, yet the Holy Spirit was present, brooding and waiting for the command of God. When the command came, "Let there be light," the Holy Spirit activated what had been decreed. Light came and the darkness fled. This is a powerful truth, for in it we find the necessity of both the Word of God and the Holy Spirit in resurrecting anything that is in a darkened, dead and dilapidated state. This truth is needed as we intercede for those who are far from God, because the spiritually dead resemble the lifeless earth before God's command and also resemble the scattered dead bones in Ezekiel's day before God breathed upon them.

I would like to include here, in its entirety, the sixth step as it was given to me. However, before I do, I again want to emphasize that the results were almost immediate. They will work if they are worked. Even as I pen these words, I marvel that I am still witnessing the wonder of these 7 intercessory steps, because they so mightily loosened my loved one from bondage, and ushered them into their prophetic purpose. All of the glory belongs to the Most High God, Who alone is the Maker of heaven and of earth. Here, then, is the sixth step as I received it from the Lord and wrote it in my journal:

> *Next, release the power of the Holy Ghost to do mightily upon the person for: The conviction of sin, the righteousness of God and of coming judgement. Release the Holy Spirit in wisdom, revelation, knowledge and the* **FEAR OF THE LORD** *(this is the big one) so that the Holy Spirit would excite such a healthy reality of the HOLINESS OF GOD and that the person may not think on anything else or have any other thought, but that God is Holy and calls us to live and be as well.*

Step 7: Give Thanks

"Giving thanks always for all things to God the Father in the name of our Lord Jesus Christ." – Ephesians 5:20

"That I may proclaim with the voice of thanksgiving, And tell of all Your wondrous works." – Psalms 26:7

"Be anxious for nothing, but in everything by prayer and supplication, *with thanksgiving*, let your requests be made known to God." – Philippians 4:6, emphasis added

Apart from it being a polite token that expresses appreciation and gratitude, thanksgiving is a powerful prayer ally. While it is vital to remain continually thankful for the many wonderful things that the Lord has done for us, it is crucial to unlock the next level of thanksgiving that very few know about, and even fewer practice. *Thanks, in advance of an answered prayer, as if the prayer has already been answered is one of the highest expressions of faith there is.*

Once, while Jesus was traveling to Jerusalem, a group of ten lepers begged him to show them mercy. Leprosy is a highly contagious flesh eating disease which causes its victims to lose body parts and afflicts them with a foul stench. In the biblical era, it was such a ghastly disease that Jewish Old Testament Law forbade a leper from having any interaction with the rest of Jewish society. They were outcasts left to fend for themselves and beg for charity (Luke 17:11-19; Leviticus 13).

If, by miraculous intervention, or a twist of good-fate, a Jewish citizen had their leprosy healed, they were to present themselves to the Jewish priest who would perform a cleansing ceremony. After careful examination of the victim by the priest and if the leprosy was in fact dissipated, the priest would proclaim them ceremonially clean. They were then permitted back into community life. When the ten lepers begged for mercy from Jesus, they could have desired any number of merciful acts, but Jesus' response was astounding, because He commanded them, "Go show yourselves to the priests" (Luke 17:14).

If there is anything the Bible teaches us, it is that when God speaks, instant obedience to His command produces an immediate blessing. Both hearing and obeying are hand-in-glove, and they are dependent upon each other. The leprous and disfigured men obeyed, and as they were on their way to the priest—remember, a leper only went to a priest *after* they had been cleansed of the disorder, not before—they were miraculously cleansed. While in route to the priest, every sign of the disease disappeared. Their obedience to the command of the Lord paid off. Faith is very much an action word.

One of the men, a Samaritan, decided to return to Jesus rather than continue his trek to the priest along with the other nine men who were Jews. The Jews did not have fond feelings toward Samaritans, and the feelings were mutual. By the time of Jesus' ministry, they were not on speaking terms. Jews had no dealings with the Samaritans, and Samaritans were considered on par with stray dogs. Interestingly, while all of the men were plagued by leprosy, the plagues of prejudice and racism were not present. The Samaritan was permitted into the company of the nine Jews. Humiliation has a way of causing the petty issues of tradition and national pride to be done away with. When everyone is suffering, no one cares what nationality the other person is, because the needs are common.

As the Samaritan made his way back to Jesus, he did so with his voice raised in praise for the miracle that had come to him. His leprosy was cleansed, and he wanted the world to hear him declare his gratefulness for the act. By the time he returned to Jesus, he was filled with ecstasy at the fact that he would no longer have to live as an outcast. The Samaritan deified social norms that were standard among his people and the Jews. Not caring what people would think about him, he fell at the Lord's feet, and with a loud uplifted-voice, he gave Him *thanks* for his cleansing.

Jesus was utterly astounded and amazed that the Samaritan was the only one to return with a thanksgiving offering unto God, and what He said next was totally amazing. Here is the entire exchange in real time:

> "And one of them, when he saw that he was healed, turned back, and with a loud voice glorified God, And fell down on his face at his feet, giving him thanks: and he was a Samaritan. And Jesus answering said, Were there not ten cleansed? but where are the nine? There are not found that returned to give glory to God, save this stranger. And he said unto him, Arise, go thy way: thy faith hath made thee *whole.*" - Luke 17:15-19, KJV, emphasis added

I opened the seventh step by making the point that, thanks, in advance of an answered prayer, as if the prayer has already been answered, is one of the highest expressions of faith there is. I called this next level thanksgiving. It is a thanks that transcends simply being thankful for all the Lord has already done. Let us not misunderstand; there is nothing in even the simplest form of thanksgiving that shouldn't be appreciated. I will always maintain that had the Lord not done another thing beyond the Cross, we would still have cause to be thankful far beyond eternity.

A careful observation of the above text will note that we aren't told the exact nature of the Samaritan's manner of thanks, but we do know that his thanks was heartfelt. He could not contain his gratitude, and he was compelled to let it show. What we do know is that it was a profound release of faith, because what happened next is both exciting and sublime. Jesus told him to go his way, indicating that he did not need to visit the priest after all and that his faith, expressed through his thanks, had made him whole.

Unless the magnitude of the moment be missed, please allow me to explain it: The Samaritan was a leper who no doubt had lost pieces of his body—a finger, an arm, a nose or his ears—

and although he was cleansed, he was likely still disfigured, but when he returned to give thanks to God for the healing of his disease, he was able to leave whole! This means that Jesus heard in the thanksgiving of the Samaritan, not only an appreciation for what was done, but of what the Lord could also do beyond just cleansing him. The other nine men were cleansed, but their failure to return with hearty thanksgiving prevented them from receiving a further blessing. They too would have been made whole, but as it stood, only the Samaritan was given the full benefit of Jesus' power.

So it is with us. When we are done praying through the six steps that lead up to the seventh and final step, let us remember to stop and give a heartfelt thanksgiving offering, not only for all that the Lord has done, but for what He will do—as if it is done already. While the 7 Steps are able to be prayed through in around three minutes, no amount of time should be included in the seventh step. In fact, I will not add an outline for thanksgiving, because that is what should emerge from our hearts, spontaneously, through our boisterous excitement.

A final observation of the Samaritan should be pointed out. Notice the manner in which he gave his thanks. Luke records that he "fell down on his face at his feet." In chapter 7, we discovered that to fall upon the knees and touch the ground with the forehead, to the ancient people of the East, was an act of profound reverence in showing homage to a person of superior rank. When the Samaritan fell upon his face and touched Jesus' feet with his forehead, he was expressing deep respect for Him. It was the fear of the Lord at work, and it was uniquely operative in him to receive his miracle.

Let us remember to Whom we pray and offer our thanksgiving in expressing our deepest respect for Him while doing it. This will hasten the breakthrough we seek. The many benefits granted us by our God await us as we walk in King Solomon's Secret—the fear of the Lord.

The Seven Step Intercessory Prayer Outline
REPENTANCE:

Father, in the name of Jesus, I approach Your throne of grace confidently and with full assurance that You always hear me. I know that appeals for Your mercy and grace to be shown to (place the name of your loved one here) will never fall on deaf ears. I know You are always ready to answer. Therefore, I bring _____ before You, and I repent for every known and unknown violation of your Holy Word (at this point, spend time repenting and bringing before the Lord every single act of rebellion or any other thing you deem pertinent. Be sure to listen to the promptings of the Holy Spirit). Also, Lord, please forgive me for every word, action or decision that has affected _____ and their present choices. I take full responsibility for every single thing I have said or done that may have contributed to _____ present manner of living. (At this time, it would be good to repent for any and all personal sins that are contributing to your loved one's present lifestyle. Please review step 1, above, if you must.)

PETITION:

Now, Father, I ask you to save _____ from their present life choices, and give them an encounter with You that is undeniable. Cause them to have such an overwhelming encounter with You that they cannot deny what they have experienced. Please bring them to repentance and submission to Your will in receiving Jesus as their Lord and Savior. (Please feel free to write out your own personal petition here. This petition can be used, but your own, I believe, will hold more value and weight.)

STAND:

These verses are my personal favorites, and they are the very ones I used in seeing my loved one set free. I used them in the order I give them below. Please use any here that you find useful to your situation, and remember to confess them out loud, reminding the Lord of His Word. Additionally, review them from alternate translations of the Bible and remember to read before and after the verses to get a better handle on the text:

- Isaiah 49:25; Isaiah 54:13-15, 17
- Jeremiah 31:16,17; Jeremiah 29:11
- Psalm 112:1, 2
- The finished work of Calvary/the Cross. (Recounting the wonders of the Cross in prayer is a tremendous encouragement and is the basis of our relationship with the Father, Son and Holy Spirit)
- Isaiah 43:5, 6; Isaiah 49:9, 10; Isaiah 42:22 (Focus on the word *restore* in this passage – King James Version and the New King James Version)

- Joel 2:28-32
- 1 Peter 5:10
- Malachi 4:5, 6 (These verses are wonderful verses for a parent to pray concerning their relationship with their children or visa-versa)
- Galatians 4:19; Galatians 5:16

BIND:

Father, now I bind _____. I tie them to Your will, O God, concerning salvation, deliverance, freedom, righteousness, faith, hope, peace, love, victory, abundance, Your dreams and desires for them, and THE BLOOD OF JESUS (and any other good thing found in the Word of God).

SEVER:

I sever _____ from any and all foul workings of the enemy, Satan, his demons, and his agents working in and through men and women or in _____ themselves. I sever and loosen them from all curses, hexes and spells. I release them from witchcraft—control, manipulation and domination—and enchantments and charms. I cut off of them, in faith, from inner vows, generational curses, ancestral vows, sins and demon worship in the name of Jesus.

RELEASE:

Next, I release the power of the Holy Ghost to do mightily upon _____ for the conviction of sin, the righteousness of God, and of coming judgement. I release the Holy Spirit in wisdom, revelation, knowledge and the FEAR OF THE LORD (this is the big one) so that the Holy Spirit would excite such a healthy reality of the HOLINESS OF GOD, and that _____ may not think on anything else or have any other thought, but that God is Holy and calls us to live and be as well.

GIVE THANKS:

You know what to do!

Repeat this outline, daily, until you see the victory. Please guard your mouth from speaking anything other than what is in agreement with your prayers and the Word of God. If doubt or fears persist, refuse them the right to get you to speak in an unbelieving manner. Say to yourself often, "I know my Father hears me!"

Stay vigilant and resist the temptation to believe that your prayers aren't being effective. The results will come fast, and you will be amazed.

Chapter Ten
Final Thoughts on King Solomon's Secret

Jesus not only taught on the fear of God (see chapter 7), but He also lived and ministered by it. Isaiah revealed, several hundred years before Christ walked the earth, which unique *grace-gifts* He would be given by the Holy Spirit. In the eleventh chapter of the book that bears his name, Isaiah says, "The spirit of the Lord shall rest upon him, the spirit of wisdom and understanding, the spirit of counsel and might, the spirit of knowledge and of **the fear of the Lord**; And shall make him of quick understanding in the **fear of the Lord**" (Isaiah 11:2-3).

Of the six spiritual graces the Holy Spirit gave to Jesus—wisdom, understanding, counsel, might, knowledge and the fear of the Lord—only the fear of the Lord is mentioned twice. No one would ever doubt that Jesus had been granted a special grace for wisdom or understanding, but most have never stopped to consider that Jesus was granted a spiritual grace called *the fear of the Lord*. Why on earth would the son of God need the fear of the Lord?

To answer the above question, it is important that we understand that Jesus is both God and man. He is not half God and half man, like the demigods of ancient, pagan religions. No, He is all God and all man, and although He lived totally as a man without exercising His divine privileges as God, there was never a moment in His earthly ministry when He was not completely God. However, every single temptation He endured, He endured as a man. He overcame them the same way that we must, by fully trusting His father and not because He is God. He lived as a man to show those who would come after Him exactly how to live as a new creation. He depended upon the Holy Spirit just as we must (Titus 2:13; John 20:28; John 1:18; Hebrews 4:15; Hebrews 5:8).

There is no legitimate recorded evidence to suggest that Jesus performed any miracles until the Holy Spirit came to rest upon Him at His water baptism. He didn't do any ministry until He was endued with power to do it and neither can we. He did not need to be baptized because He needed cleansing. He was baptized because a good leader leads by example. So then, Jesus, being a man, needed the fear of the Lord for our sake, because without it, we cannot expect to fully thrive in His Kingdom on earth (Matthew 3:14-15).

The Secret to Clean Living

In discussing the beautiful revelation of the fear of God, I have seen people become perplexed, because they assume, wrongly, that I am encouraging them to muster up the fear of God for themselves. There seems to be some confusion as to how the fear of God comes to us and works in our lives. We can no more work up an attitude of the fear of God than we can the grace, love, mercy or peace of God. I set out to write this book in order to assuage some of the difficulties around this great truth, and after all, if God saw no need for it, He would not have included it in the Scriptures. Avoiding it because we don't understand it will do us a profound disservice.

If the fear of God is missing in us, then all we need to do is ask the Lord for it. If, for example, we were lacking God's peace, we would go to the Lord and ask Him why our peaceful disposition has been interrupted, because we know that it is our wonderful right and privilege to abide in and dwell under it. Once we have concluded why our peace was disrupted, we can then rectify the matter and ask God to restore His peace to us. Next, we need only to receive from Him, what has been freely given to us through His Son. Our peace will be restored when we seek for its return, and the process is the same in the absence of the fear of God—we should seek for its return (John 14:1, 27; Matthew 7:7).

There is a sad assumption about the fear of God, specifically the belief that it is something we control ourselves. I have heard ministers of the Gospel tell people living in sin and rebellion that their problem is that they simply do not fear God. While it may be true that they need the fear of God, it will do them no good to tell them what's missing without helping them understand how to get it. They will likely believe that it is up to them to acquire it without the aid of heaven. No person can simply turn the fear of God on and off. They can no more provide themselves with the fear of God than they could the peace of God, because it is not theirs to give, for it belongs to God, and only He can give it.

When we see the words *"the grace **of** God,"* we automatically know that the grace belongs to God, and if we want it, we had better go to the Source of grace. However, when we see the words *"the fear **of** God,"* we do not initially draw the same conclusion. Just as God is in possession of His *grace*, He is also in possession of His *fear*, and if we are lacking it, then we know from

Whom to get it. But, how do we know if the fear of God is lacking in our lives? The answer is simple: are we living a morally clean life?

"The fear of the Lord," King Solomon wrote, "is clean." Another translation replaces *clean* with *pure*. One of the primary functions of the *Fear of God* is that it works thoroughly at cleansing our lives from every iniquitous defilement. *The Fear of the Lord* is an expert purifier, and this is its central assignment, but not its only one (Psalm 19:9).

A morally clean life is not to be confused with a sin-free life. We will always have a struggle with our flesh, and, from time-to-time, we will sin. We may hate it, but we will still fall into it. Whether by thought, word or deed, we are sure to come up short every now and then. However, the difference with a morally clean life and sinning occasionally is that sin patterns are not dominating us. In other words, we do not wake up daily looking for opportunities to sin. Sadly, many Christians find themselves bound by immoral living. They beg for forgiveness when they fail, make promises to never again do the heinous act, and then repeat it, with the vicious cycle starting over. There is a better way (1 John 1:8; 3:8-9; Hebrew 6:1).

The fear of God is designed to liberate us by cleaning us up. There is no path, back alley, road or highway in our heart and mind that the fear of God will not go through, and like a street sweeper, once it is received and released into our lives, it will work powerfully at cleaning up the debris that has been littering our lives. All we need to do is recognize that it is missing, and if there is a present sin pattern at work, then it *is* absent or at least diminished. If it is missing, then we must ask God to restore it to our lives. He has it, and all we have to do is go get it from Him. We should want the fear of God operational in our lives. The following verse is a potent reminder of just how effective the fear of God is in helping us maintain a morally pure and holy life before God:

> "Therefore, having these promises, beloved, let us cleanse ourselves from all filthiness of the flesh and spirit, perfecting holiness in the fear of God." – 2 Corinthians 7:1

Two other misunderstandings occur when discussing the fear of God. The first is that it promotes a *works-based* Christianity, which leads to *legalism*. I am not entirely sure how this is derived when a teaching on the fear of God is given, but I will address it, because I have had people challenge me with these two assumptions.

First, *works-based* Christianity is a performance focused approach to serving God. Essentially, it says that the more a person reads their Bible, attends church or prays, the greater favor with God they will possess. If there is ever a steep drop off in the performances, then so too will God's favor diminish. Secondly, and along with this perverted view of Christianity, is the idea that one's performance will determine their level of faith for believing God to do things through them. The more they do for God, the more He will do through them is the thinking. While all of the above disciplines will enhance a person's knowledge of God and promote a healthier relationship with Him, they will not get Him to love them any more than He already does. He will never love us based on our performance, and He works mightily through those who believe Him to do so, and not because they have earned the right for Him to do so.

The natural outworking of a performance based mindset is *legalism*. Legalism seeks to impose rigid requirements and demands upon the self, and it typically frowns down upon others who do not do the same things that the legalist is doing to remain righteous and holy before God. An example of this comes from my own life. I dislike alcohol in every form. It is a personal conviction of my own that I am not to put alcohol into my body. I have no desire for it, and I do not wish that anyone would drink it. The reasons for this personal belief are many, but the main reason has to do with my former manner of living. Alcohol reminds me of my past before I came alive to God. However, there is always the danger lurking that I might believe that I am better than Christians who imbibe, and I admit I have, in the past, fallen into this trap. However, I have learned that I cannot, in good conscience, tell anyone that drinking alcohol is a sin, because the Bible never says that it is. While there are plenty of verses in the Bible that deal with the negative nature of consuming alcohol, the Bible only says that *drunkenness will not inherit the Kingdom of God*. The problem is that each person is left to determine for themselves, along with the Holy Spirit, what a drunken threshold means for them. As much as I can warn people against the ravaging effect that alcohol has had on countless souls, all I can do is pray that they will ultimately come to the same conviction I have about it—that it should be avoided. I do not drink so that God will be better pleased with me. Instead, I do not drink because He has removed the desire for it from me, and those who do occasionally consume alcohol are no less loved by Him (Galatians 5:21; Ephesians 5:18).

If a *works-based* lifestyle or *legalism* ensues after hearing a message or teaching on the fear of God, it is not because the fear of God naturally promotes them; it is because there has been a misunderstanding that the fear of God is somehow a *work* of our own. The fear of God is not a *work*; it is the outworking of the grace of God. It is a free gift to help us maintain a standard of conduct before God that is well pleasing to Him. The beauty of it is that we don't even need to try to be moral, because the fear of God, when allowed, will do the work through us. It is easy to live a life that is pleasing to the Lord:

> "Therefore, since we are receiving a kingdom which cannot be shaken, let us have **grace**, by which we may serve God acceptably with reverence and **godly fear**. For our God is a consuming fire." - Hebrews 12:28-29

Both grace and righteousness are free gifts from God, based solely on Jesus' completed work on the Cross and His fulfillment of the Law of Moses. When we place our faith and trust in Him and what He did for us, we are made righteous. As well, we are made holy in and through Him. Of course, we are called to *live-out* a holy life and are commissioned to remain purged from every violation of our new nature. This is primarily the reason why we need the fear of God to be functional in our lives. Without the fear of God, a person begins to lose their way. They begin to embrace things that they once felt were a detriment to them, and while the downward spiral begins slowly, it speeds up until the current gets harder to break free from (Romans 3-6; Matthew 5:17; Jeremiah 2:19; 1Peter 1:15).

The Secret to Shunning Evil

Another function of the fear of God is to cause us to *hate evil*. When the fear of the Lord is operating at peak capacity, there will be a natural aversion toward evil. All the preaching in the world won't cause a man to hate evil as effectively as the fear of God will. The repulsion of wickedness and evil can't be had from the mouth of a preacher unless the preacher himself is walking in it. His preaching cannot excite what he does not own for himself. When a man or woman of God is set ablaze with the fiery presence of the fear of God, they will inspire their hearers to reject evil at every turn (Exodus 18:17-21).

When the fear of God is upon a people, they will not need to have evil defined for them; they will just know what evil is. Gone will be the debates about what is allowable and acceptable before God, because each will begin to walk out their *own* salvation with "fear and trembling." Sadly, I see many within modern Christian circles attempting to redefine God's moral standards even at the expense of reinterpreting the Word of God. When the fear of God is working, eyes begin to see with greater clarity what is good and acceptable before Him (Proverbs 8:13; Psalm 2:11; Philippians 2:12; Romans 12:2).

There aren't many evils that a Christian could do to cause God to distance Himself from them, but pride is one of those evils. God has made it His prerogative to oppose the proud. A prideful person makes God their enemy. Conversely, there are some things that draw the attention, compassion and care of God quickly and being humble is one of them. When the fear of the Lord is at work in a person, it will ferret out pride and its close cousin, arrogance, and promote a healthy humility (James 4:6; Proverbs 8:13).

Pride was at work in Satan when he failed to takeover God's throne. His rebellion was fueled by it. Pride is satanic at every level, and for this reason, God hates its presence in His children, so He completely sets His face against the proud. Pride is a subtle creature, and it isn't easily discerned. In fact, those living in pride are usually the last to know, yet the fear of the Lord knows how to find it, expose it, and drive it out (Isaiah 14:12-17; James 4:6; 1 Peter 5:5).

There are various forms of pride that are subtle, yet have the appearance of being acceptable, but are actually dangerous to a healthy walk with God. Things like racial, ethnic and national pride end up being hazardous because they tend to foster the preference of one group over another. It is not necessarily wrong to have love for country or heritage, but we must never allow ourselves to look down on other people from different expressions and experiences that are different than our own. The fear of God will always promote a humble disposition and never one that prizes race over love for our neighbor. The fear of God will never drive us away from the essential command to love one another. Instead, it will promote it.

Spiritual-pride (also called religious-pride) is among the most dangerous types of pride there is. Those weighted down with spiritual-pride look down upon and think less of people who do not worship God in the manner that they do. They prize and promote non-essential elements of the Bible and reject others who do not hold to the same dogmas.

Keep in mind, *essential* doctrines are those in which the entirety of the Christian faith are hinged, and they must be believed to be called a Christian. These include: the virgin birth of Christ,

His sinless life, His death, and His resurrection from the dead. *Non-essential* doctrines may be important, but they are not mandatory for a relationship with God or for eternal salvation. These include: tithes and offerings, styles and forms of worship, and what day to worship on, to name a few.

There is little doubt that God has had a plan to use varying Christian denominations in advancing the faith, but rather than working together and celebrating uniqueness, some denominations have taken the stance that theirs is the right and only way to worship. I have, on more than one occasion, been told that the Catholic faith is the true and only church, and anything outside of it is anathema and heretical. In essence, they were saying that I was misleading people and preaching a false gospel. I am not suggesting that the Vatican is driving this narrative, but I don't think much has been done to discourage it either.

On the other hand, I have had my protestant friends and brethren tell me that the Catholic church is a cult and that the Pope would be the future anti-Christ of Revelation. Since I have family and friends that worship as Catholics, I have been much pained to hear such rhetoric. I have seen in Catholics a deep love for Christ, strong devotion to Him, and a bold confession. I have even marveled at their dogged commitment to social justice for the societally downtrodden.

Making blanket statements about fellow believers who worship differently than we do does little to foster healthy inter-Christian relationships, and it will hinder the advance of our faith. Jesus promised that if we loved one another, then it would be the greatest demonstration of our relationship with Him there could be. Spiritual-pride keeps more people out of heaven than it brings into it, and the fear of the Lord must be welcomed if we are going to see it deposed from our denominational contexts (John 13:35).

The fear of the Lord has a way of revealing the awesomeness of Calvary to us. By showing us our personal and individual sin laid upon Jesus, the fear of God makes it hard for us to look down on any one, especially a confessing brother or sister who may worship differently than we do. The fear of God, when it is truly working, makes much of Jesus' finished work, and reminds us of our wretchedness outside of it. Our right position before God, in Christ, is only magnified when we understand our distance from God outside of Christ. We cannot snub another believer, whatever their worship persuasion may be, when the fear of the Lord is at work in us. By aid of the fear of God, we will view ourselves primarily from a position of God's grace, and not through some special commissioning of heaven. We were not saved or called due to any personal merit of our own, and no denomination will ever have the corner on God. We are better than no one else, nor were we more worthy of saving than anyone else.

The Secret of Great Leadership

Christian leaders would do well to continuously ask the Lord to endue them, by the Holy Spirit, with the fear of the Lord. Satan often tempts those called to serve the Lord's heritage into believing that the ministry they are occupied with only exists because of them. The result of such misguided thinking is a belief that God's people are simply present to serve their personal interests. Leaders who have fallen victim to this way of believing end up building their own kingdoms, not the Lord's. However, when the fear of the Lord is in operation in a leader's life and when he or she is constantly monitoring its level of activity in them, the enemy will be hard-pressed to get them to fall into his snare.

Nothing saddens the Lord more than church leaders who abuse and oppress His people. Christian leadership is not secular leadership, but often enough, leaders within the church make the mistake of taking their leadership cues from the secular marketplace. Not all secular leadership is bad and much can be learned from it, but secular leadership can, at times, be dictatorial and demanding, relying on pleasing leaders and upon performance nearly 100% of the time. Leadership that is Christ centered and Christ driven must always seek to serve and guide the Lord's people into becoming mature and productive Kingdom citizens. This cannot be done with threats, harsh demands, or reprisals when a Christian is struggling, for example, with faithfulness and consistency. A Christian leader should be tender and patient, not pushy or rude. The fear of God is an invaluable partner to leaders who hope to continuously please their Master in their service to His people, and they will be healthier and happier when their leaders understand the necessity of walking in His fear (John 21:15-17; 2 Timothy 2:24-26; Ephesians 4:11-16).

No worker in Christ's household should ever use His people for their own personal benefit. They should not burden them with guilt, condemnation or shame, especially during times when the leader's own needs or the needs of a ministry are going unmet. Every Christian leader must depend solely upon the Lord for His provision, and manipulating, cajoling and haranguing parishioners for money will only garner the Lord's ire. The Lord's people are never to be merchandised (1 Peter 5:1-4).

A biblical leader named Nehemiah understood this fact. Nehemiah was a high official in the court of the Persian empire, and He had a pretty cushy government job, which came with a residence within the protective walls of the capital city's citadel. The Jews of the Judea region of southern Israel had been living in Babylon since the days when they were taken captive by the Babylonian king, Nebuchadnezzar. Jerusalem, their capital city and center of worship, had been completely destroyed by Nebuchadnezzar, and their temple, built by Solomon, was not spared in the overthrow (Nehemiah 1:1-2; 2 Chronicles 36; Daniel 1:1).

Seventy years after their captivity, the Jews were granted permission to return back to Jerusalem. The city was desolate, in total ruins, and lacked leadership. In those days, a city without a protective wall was frequently overrun, and its residents were susceptible to habitual burglary. The Jews did their best to fortify themselves, but were met with continuing failure. About ninety years after the first Jews returned from exile in Babylon, Nehemiah became burdened to see his homeland healed and restored. After a season of prayer, he was given leave by the king to go to Jerusalem and repair the walls, and he was made the city's governor (Jeremiah 25:8-12, 29:10-14; Ezra 1-6; Nehemiah 5:14).

When Nehemiah arrived in the city, it was a politically insignificant locale, but to him it was special, because it was his people's eternal capital given to them by God. His brother Hanani had gone back to Jerusalem before him and had sent word of the city's disrepair. Nehemiah was deeply troubled and saddened by the report. He no doubt knew the prophecies about what Jerusalem and his people would become, and he longed to see the place positioned for the eventual coming of his Messiah (Nehemiah 1:2, 2:1-2; Psalm 137:5; Isaiah 62:7).

As Nehemiah set about to repair the outer fortification walls of the city, he was met with continual opposition and aggressive threats. He worked harder, day-and-night. He led with courage and tenacity. The people of the land had grown accustomed to subjugating Jerusalem's residents, and they didn't like that Nehemiah had come to bring order and a biblically based rule of law. They wanted to keep the status quo.

Sadly, Nehemiah even found that the governors of Jerusalem before him had oppressed the Jewish residents by laying heavy financial burdens upon them. Nehemiah was determined to govern with the Lord's heart, and this is what he said when he discovered that the previous leadership had been fleecing the city's residents:

> "Moreover, from the time that I was appointed to be their governor in the land of Judah, from the twentieth year until the thirty-second year of King Artaxerxes, twelve years, neither I nor my brothers ate the governor's provisions. But the former governors who were before me laid burdens on the people, and took from them bread and wine, besides forty shekels of silver. Yes, even their servants bore rule over the people, but I did not do so, **because of the fear of God**. Indeed, I also continued the work on this wall, and we did not buy any land. All my servants were gathered there for the work. And at my table were one hundred and fifty Jews and rulers, besides those who came to us from the nations around us. Now that which was prepared daily was one ox and six choice sheep. Also fowl were prepared for me, and once every ten days an abundance of all kinds of wine. **Yet in spite**

of this I did not demand the governor's provisions, because the bondage was heavy on this people. Remember me, my God, for good, according to all that I have done for this people." - Nehemiah 5:14-19, emphasis added

I think it is safe to suggest that a leader who refuses to acknowledge the need to walk in the fear of God, as Nehemiah did, will eventually lose their way. I am amazed, not so much that Nehemiah wielded immense compassion toward the affliction of his compatriots, but that the compassion was driven by the fear of God. He wanted to do right by the people of God, because He feared the God of his people. The fear of God made him compassionate, but it also made him courageous. Leadership must be courageous, but it is never exemplified in expressions of power, but in expressions of empowerment. Real leadership inspires others to do more than they thought they could and to go further than they once believed possible. Nehemiah understood this, and he motivated and inspired his people to help him complete the task of completing the city wall within a staggering fifty-two-day period. His leadership set the stage for more exiles to return and for God to begin ramping up the region for the coming of Jesus (Nehemiah 6:15).

The greatest leaders of the Bible—Abraham, Solomon, Paul and Jesus—all possessed, like Nehemiah, the fear of God. Even Solomon, who lost it and found it again, could have never done the great things he did for the Lord without the Lord's fear. It is possible that both Abraham and Paul would have missed their calling and would have never been given insight into the elite strategies of heaven had they not walked in the fear of the Lord.

My Secret Hope for YOU!

If you desire to do things for the Lord that have never been done and to be used by Him in unique ways that others may only be dreaming of, then I urge you to begin asking the Lord, daily, to release another level of the fear of the Lord in you. This may seem counterproductive on the surface, but it may be one of the most underused prayer requests there is. Most would think that if they desired to be used by God, then they should simply ask Him to use them, but there is a better way as the following verse shows:

> "The secret of the Lord is with those who fear Him, And He will show them His covenant." - Psalm 25:14

God, desires to reveal His strategies, plans and purposes to those who will walk in His fear. He holds secrets regarding His eternal plan and covenant for mankind that He cannot share with everyone, but perhaps you desire to be one of the people He can confide in. If you are, then I urge you today to begin asking Him to cause, by the Holy Spirit, to make the fear of the Lord come and rest upon you. My hope is that you will desire the fear of the Lord as much as you desire anything else in your life!

If you decide to ask the Lord to walk in *King Solomon's Secret*, you will be amazed at the higher levels of wisdom you will begin operating in. Your worship will deepen, your core life motivators will align themselves with God's will, and the intensity of your intercession will be amped up. You will find a renewed zeal to see your loved ones come to the saving knowledge of Jesus Christ. You will find yourself among God's elite class of Christians.

— *Paul Anthony González* —

Here is my prayer for you:

"Father, in the name of Jesus, I ask You to cause all who have held this book and read its words to begin walking in the fear of God. I pray, Lord, that You will cause them to walk in higher levels of wisdom, deepen their worship, align their will with Yours, intensify their intercession, and give them a renewed zeal to see their loved ones saved from a destructive path. Raise them up to do wonderful works for Your glory, I pray—amen and amen."

May the Lord bless you as you seek Him and abide in *King Solomon's Secret*!

About the Author

Paul Anthony Gonzalez is a pastor, speaker, and Bible teacher with 29 years of church leadership experience. In that time, he has founded two churches and held the position of preaching pastor at the historical Belmont Church in the heart of Midtown in Nashville, TN. While his love and passion for people are evident through his pastoral work, it is his calling as a father and husband that brings him his greatest satisfaction and joy. Paul and his wife Amy share ten children, 5 boys and 5 girls, and reside in middle Tennessee.

For more information, to share how ***King Solomon's Secret*** has blessed you, or to invite Paul to speak at your church or event please contact him at paul@awakeningnasville.org

www.ingramcontent.com/pod-product-compliance
Lightning Source LLC
Chambersburg PA
CBHW070142100426
42743CB00013B/2804